W9-AUO-209

OLD

AND

NEW

POEMS

POETRY BY DONALD HALL

Exiles and Marriages (1955)
The Dark Houses (1958)
A Roof of Tiger Lilies (1964)
The Alligator Bride (1969)
The Yellow Room (1971)
The Town of Hill (1975)
Kicking the Leaves (1978)
The Happy Man (1986)
The One Day (1988)

OLD AND NEW POEMS

DONALD HALL

✦ ✦ ✦

TICKNOR
& FIELDS
NEW YORK
1990

For information about permission to reproduce selections
from this book, write to Permissions, Ticknor & Fields,
215 Park Avenue South, New York, New York 10003.

Library of Congress Cataloging-in-Publication Data

Hall, Donald, date.
   [Poems.   Selections]
   Old and new poems / Donald Hall.
     p.   cm.
   ISBN 0-89919-926-7   ISBN 0-89919-954-2 (pbk.)
   I. Title.
  PS3515.A315204   1990
  811'.54 — dc20   90-31087
                         CIP

Printed in the United States of America

BP 10 9 8 7 6 5 4 3 2 1

Book design by Anne Chalmers

The following poems previously appeared in *The Happy Man,* copyright © 1981,
1982, 1983, 1984, 1986 by Donald Hall, reprinted by permission of Random
House, Inc.: Great Day in the Cows' House, Whip-poor-will, Scenic View, New
Animals, The Rocker, The Henyard Round, Twelve Seasons, Mr. Wakeville on
Interstate 90, Sums, The Revolution, Old Timers' Day (Couplet), The Baseball
Players, My Friend Felix, Merle Bascom's .22, A Sister on the Tracks, For an
Exchange of Rings, The Impossible Marriage, Acorns, Granite and Grass, A Sister
by the Pond, The Day I Was Older.

A number of poems previously appeared in the following publications: *American
Poetry Review:* Notes for Nobody, This Poem. *Arete:* Speeches. *The Atlantic
Monthly:* Material. *The Boston Review:* Persistence of 1937. *Boulevard:* Tubes.
Brief Lives (W. Ewert). *Four Stories* (Ives Street Press): Carlotta's Confession,
Cider 5¢ A Glass, Edward's Anecdote. *The Gettysburg Review:* Praise for Death.
The Hudson Review: Carlotta's Confession. *The Iowa Review:* The Coffee Cup,
Valley of Morning. *The New Criterion:* Cider 5¢ A Glass, Tomorrow. *The New
Yorker:* The Clown, Moon Clock, Six Naps in One Day. *Ploughshares:* Match.
The Reaper: Edward's Anecdote. *The Sewanee Review:* A Grace, Maundy Thurs-
day's Candles. *Times Literary Supplement:* Our Walk in Yorkshire. *The Virginia
Quarterly Review:* Milkers Broken Up.

for Emily
for Allison

CONTENTS

1947–1953

OLD HOME WEEK   3

WEDDING PARTY   3

LOVE IS LIKE SOUNDS   4

A CHILD'S GARDEN   4

SOME ODDITIES   5

SEPTEMBER ODE   6

PASSAGE TO WORSHIP   7

EXILE   8

AT DELPHI   11

THE COLUMNS OF THE PARTHENON   12

THE LONE RANGER   12

A FRIEND REVISITED   13

ELEGY FOR WESLEY WELLS   14

1954–1958

MY SON MY EXECUTIONER   19

CONDUCT AND WORK   19

THE RED BRANCH   20

CHRISTMAS EVE IN WHITNEYVILLE   21

THE HOLE   23

COPS AND ROBBERS   23

THE SLEEPING GIANT   24

DANCERS   25

NO DEPOSIT   26

THE BODY POLITIC   27

A SECOND STANZA   28

TO THE LOUD WIND 29

ABROAD THOUGHTS FROM HOME 29

FATHERS AND SONS 30

A SMALL FIG TREE 31

JE SUIS UNE TABLE 32

SHUDDER 32

BY THE EXETER RIVER 33

THE UMBRELLA 34

THE HUT OF THE MAN ALONE 35

OYSTERS AND HERMITS 36

1934 37

WAITING ON THE CORNERS 38

THE THREE MOVEMENTS 39

SESTINA 41

A SET OF SEASONS 42

"THE SCREAM" 43

"MARAT'S DEATH" 44

"THE KISS" 44

"BETWEEN THE CLOCK AND THE BED" 45

CHRIST CHURCH MEADOWS 46

THE CLOWN 47

PRESIDENT AND POET 48

RELIGIOUS ARTICLES 49

THE FOUNDATIONS OF AMERICAN INDUSTRY 50

THE WIDOWS 51

MR. AND MRS. BILLINGS 52

THE FAMILY 53

THE GROWN-UPS 55

1959–1963

THE LONG RIVER 59

THE SNOW 59

THE FARM 61

THE POEM 62

THE TREE AND THE CLOUD 62

THE IDEA OF FLYING 63

THE MOON 64

THE SUN 65

THE CHILD 65

THE KILL 66

THE SEA 67

WELLS 67

THE WRECKAGE 68

AN AIRSTRIP IN ESSEX *1960* 69

NEW HAMPSHIRE 70

SOUTHWEST OF BUFFALO 70

SELF-PORTRAIT AS A BEAR 71

MYCENAE 72

ON A HORSE CARVED IN WOOD 72

JEALOUS LOVERS 73

SLEEPING 74

"INTERNAL AND EXTERNAL FORMS" 74

"KING AND QUEEN" 75

"RECLINING FIGURE" 76

DIGGING 76

"O FLODDEN FIELD" 77

COLD WATER 78

THE OLD PILOT 80

BEAU OF THE DEAD 80

A VILLAGE IN EAST ANGLIA 81

LETTER TO AN ENGLISH POET 84

STUMP 86

IN THE KITCHEN OF THE OLD HOUSE 88

THE DAYS 89

1966–1969

THE MAN IN THE DEAD MACHINE 93

THE CORNER 93

SWAN 94

THE ALLIGATOR BRIDE 96

THE GRAVE THE WELL 97

SEW 98

OLD HOUSES 98

PICTURES OF PHILIPPA 99

THE COAL FIRE 100

THE BLUE WING 101

THE REPEATED SHAPES 102

WOOLWORTH'S 102

APPLES 103

THE TABLE 104

MOUNT KEARSARGE 106

1970–1974

GOLD 109

WATERS 109

THE YOUNG WATCH US 110

THE DUMP 110

NOSE 111

NO COLOR MAN 112

STONES 112

THE HIGH PASTURE 113

STORIES 114

TO A WATERFOWL 115

POEM WITH ONE FACT 116

THE GREEN SHELF 118

FÊTE 119

THE PRESIDENTIAD 119

ELEANOR'S LETTERS 120

THE RAISIN 121

TRANSCONTINENT 122

WHITE APPLES 123

THE TOWN OF HILL 123

1975–1978

MAPLE SYRUP 127

THE TOY BONE 129

ILLUSTRATION 130

ADULTERY AT FORTY 131

O CHEESE 131

KICKING THE LEAVES 132

EATING THE PIG 135

WOLF KNIFE 139

PHOTOGRAPHS OF CHINA 141

ON REACHING THE AGE OF TWO HUNDRED 143

FLIES 144

OX CART MAN 147

STONE WALLS 148

OLD ROSES 153

TRAFFIC 153

THE BLACK-FACED SHEEP 156

NAMES OF HORSES 158

1979–1986

GREAT DAY IN THE COWS' HOUSE 163

THE HENYARD ROUND 166

WHIP-POOR-WILL 168

NEW ANIMALS 169

THE ROCKER 170

TWELVE SEASONS 171

SCENIC VIEW 175

SUMS 176

THE REVOLUTION 177

OLD TIMERS' DAY 177

THE BASEBALL PLAYERS 178

GRANITE AND GRASS 179

A SISTER ON THE TRACKS 181

A SISTER BY THE POND 182

THE DAY I WAS OLDER 186

ACORNS 187

FOR AN EXCHANGE OF RINGS 188

THE IMPOSSIBLE MARRIAGE 189

MR. WAKEVILLE ON INTERSTATE 90   190
MY FRIEND FELIX   191
MERLE BASCOM'S .22   192

1987–1990

CIDER 5¢ A GLASS   197
EDWARD'S ANECDOTE   202
CARLOTTA'S CONFESSION   204
BRIEF LIVES   208
OUR WALK IN YORKSHIRE   209
A CAROL   209
A GRACE   210
MAUNDY THURSDAY'S CANDLES   210
MATERIAL   211
MOON CLOCK   212
MATCH   212
PERSISTENCE OF 1937   213
MILKERS BROKEN UP   213
NOTES FOR NOBODY   214
SIX NAPS IN ONE DAY   216
TOMORROW   217
TUBES   218
VALLEY OF MORNING   221
THE COFFEE CUP   222
SPEECHES   223
THIS POEM   227
PRAISE FOR DEATH   229

NOTES ON *Old and New Poems*   237
INDEX OF TITLES AND FIRST LINES   239

1947–1953

———————

OLD HOME WEEK

Old man remembers to old man
   How bat struck ball upon this plain,
Seventy years ago, before
   The batter's box washed out in rain.

WEDDING PARTY

The pock-marked player of the accordion
Empties and fills his squeeze box in the corner,
Kin to the tiny man who pours champagne,
Kin to the caterer. These solemn men,
Amid the sounds of silk and popping corks,
Stand like pillars. And the white bride
Moves through the crowd as a chaired relic moves.

We are the guest invited yesterday,
Friend to the bride's rejected suitor, come
On sudden visit unexpectedly.
And so we chat, on best behavior, with
The Uncle, Aunt, and unattractive girl;
And watch the summer twilight slide away
As thunder gathers head to end the day.

Now all at once the pock-marked player grows
Immense and terrible beside the bride
Whose marriage withers to a rind of years
And curling photographs in a dry box;
And in the storm that hurls upon the room
Above the crowd he holds his breathing box
That only empties, fills, empties, fills.

3

LOVE IS LIKE SOUNDS

Late snow fell this early morning of spring.
At dawn I rose from bed, restless, and looked
Out of my window, to wonder if there the snow
Fell outside your bedroom, and you watching.

I played my game of solitaire. The cards
Came out the same the third time through the deck.
The game was stuck. I threw the cards together,
And watched the snow that could not do but fall.

Love is like sounds, whose last reverberations
Hang on the leaves of strange trees, on mountains
As distant as the curving of the earth,
Where the snow hangs still in the middle of the air.

A CHILD'S GARDEN

I'm sure I can't remember where, but some
Where in this jungle I have lost the key
That locks the door of Grandfather's walled garden
Where he and I, before he died, would play,

And he would sing about the funny sun
That circled over the garden every day.
But then he died. I didn't know a thing
Of what a grown-up would have done, and so

I ran away when April ate him up,
Our dog. And now the door is shut, and just

The walls are all I see, and sometimes I
Don't know if there's a garden there at all.

The animals just look at me. I bit
A rat to death three days ago and ate him.
A tiger has been padding all today
Behind me, and I cannot sleep at all.

I cannot sleep at all, and what is worse
Yesterday I tried to talk again
Just like I did with Grampa, but my voice
Was only grunts. I made no words at all.

SOME ODDITIES

The hugy spider stooping through the door
Rushes to kiss me, but I am not there;
I have retreated through the floor
And hear him flounder at the empty air;
I sit in my concealment, smiling
To hear him weep and swear;
And now the keepers come with candy,
He
Will need no more beguiling.
These sentimental beasts are all the same,
Stupid and loving, quick to kiss or cry;
That dragon last week, with his game
Of burning love-words on the midnight sky;
Or any unicornish creature:
Two heads or just one eye.
I wish they wouldn't come and slobber,
For
I'm through with oddities of nature.

SEPTEMBER ODE

And now September burns the careful tree
That builds each year the leaf and bark again
With solemn care and rounded certainty
That nothing lives which seasons do not mend.

But we were strangers in that formal wood
Those years ago, and we have grown to change,
Ignorant of the fury of the blood,
And we have tasted what is new and strange.

This new September's pilgrimage is made,
Remembering that season of the mind
When we were Tamburlaines of leaf and shade
And Alexanders of the lusty wind.

But only seasons spin around the tree
In winter thick and summer narrow bark;
The person learns a changing cruelty;
Possessions cumber us from going back.

Only the young are really pitiable
Who walk from high school past my cluttered room,
Who live in last night's party, and who tell
What happened in the darkened living room.

That innocence is only negative
And innocence is only not to know
That all intensity is curative
In the disease of love we undergo.

This room is cluttered with the truth of years,
Possessions of the unreturning blood.
And innocence possesses only fears
Of parting from the comfort of the wood.

Wealthy with love and fruitful memory,
I pity only those who have no guilt.
It is the structure of complicity,
The monument experience has built.

The tree is burning on the autumn noon
That builds each year the leaf and bark again.
Though frost will strip it raw and barren soon,
The rounding season will restore and mend.

Yet people are not mended, but go on,
Accumulating memory and love.
And so the wood we used to know is gone,
Because the years have taught us that we move.

We have moved on, the Tamburlaines of then,
To different Asias of our plundering.
And though we sorrow not to know again
A land or face we loved, yet we are king.

The young are never robbed of innocence
But given gold of love and memory.
We live in wealth whose bounds exceed our sense,
And when we die are full of memory.

PASSAGE TO WORSHIP

Those several times she cleaved my dark,
Silver and homeless, I from sleep
Rose up, and tried to touch or mark
That storied personage with deep
Unmotivated love. My days were full,
My halting days were full of rage,

Resisting in my heart the pull
Toward reverence or pilgrimage.
But now this blinding sheeted bird
Or goddess stood at my bed's head,
Demanding worship, and no word
But honoring the steadfast dead.

EXILE

Each of us waking to the window's light
Has found the curtains changed, our pictures gone;
Our furniture has vanished in the night
And left us to an unfamiliar dawn;
Even the contours of the room are strange
And everything is change.
Waking, our minds construct of memory
What figure stretched beside us, or what voice
Shouted to pull us from our luxury—
And all the mornings leaning to our choice.

To put away — both child and murderer —
The toys we played with just a month ago,
That wisdom come, and make our progress sure,
Began our exile with our lust to grow.
(Remembering a train I tore apart
Because it knew my heart.)
We move to move, and this perversity
Betrays us into loving only loss.
We seek betrayal. When we cross the sea,
It is the distance from our past we cross.

Not only from the intellectual child
Time has removed us, but unyieldingly

Cuts down the groves in which our Indians filed
And where the black of pines was mystery.
(I walked the streets of where I lived and grew,
And all the streets were new.)
The room of love is always rearranged.
Someone has torn the corner of a chair
So that the past we call upon has changed,
The scene deprived by an intruding tear.

Exiled by death from people we have known,
We are reduced again by years, and try
To call them back and clothe the barren bone,
Not to admit that people ever die.
(A boy who talked and read and grew with me
Fell from a maple tree.)
But we are still alone, who love the dead,
And always miss their action's character,
Caught in the cage of living, visited
By no faint ghosts, by no gray men that were.

In years, and in the numbering of space,
Moving away from what we grew to know,
We stray like paper blown from place to place,
Impelled by every element to go.
(I think of haying on an August day,
Forking the stacks of hay.)
We can remember trees and attitudes
That foreign landscapes do not imitate;
They grow distinct within the interludes
Of memory beneath a stranger state.

The favorite toy was banished, and our act
Was banishment of the self; then growing, we
Betrayed the girls we loved, for our love lacked
Self-knowledge of its real perversity.
(I loved her, but I told her I did not,
And grew, and then forgot.)

9

It was mechanical, and in our age,
That cruelty should be our way of speech;
Our movement is a single pilgrimage,
Never returning; action does not teach.

In isolation from our present love
We make her up, consulting memory,
Imagining to watch her image move
On daily avenues across a sea.
(All day I saw her daydreamed figure stand
Out of the reach of hand.)
Each door and window is a spectral frame
In which her shape is for the moment found;
Each lucky scrap of paper bears her name,
And half-heard phrases imitate its sound.

Imagining, by exile kept from fact,
We build of distance mental rock and tree,
And make of memory creative act,
Persons and worlds no waking eye can see.
(From lacking her, I built her new again,
And loved the image then.)
The manufactured country is so green
The eyes of sleep are blinded by its shine;
We spend our lust in that imagined scene
But never wake to cross its borderline.

No man can knock his human fist upon
The door built by his mind, or hear the voice
He meditated come again if gone;
We live outside the country of our choice.
(I wanted X. When X moved in with me,
I could not wait to flee.)
Our humanness betrays us to the cage
Within whose limits each is free to walk,
But where no one can hear our prayers or rage
And none of us can break the walls to talk.

Exiled by years, by death no dream conceals,
By worlds that must remain unvisited,
And by the wounds that growing never heals,
We are as solitary as the dead,
Wanting to king it in that perfect land
We make and understand.
And in this world whose pattern is unmade,
Phases of splintered light and shapeless sand,
We shatter through our motions and evade
Whatever hand might reach and touch our hand.

AT DELPHI

At Delphi where the eagles climb
Over Parnassus' naked head
I saw the burden of the dead,
    Perfected out of time.

I met a donkey and a man
Who carted olive branches through
The marble wastes where little grew
    And once great runners ran.

The temple where the priestess told
Young Oedipus whom he would kill
Lay dissipated on the hill,
    Where grass grew faint as mold.

No priestess spoke. I heard one sound.
The donkey's sure and nerveless plod
Past ruined columns of a god
    Made dactyls on the ground.

THE COLUMNS OF THE PARTHENON

White bone in the yellow flats of sun,
bone in the flutes of rain.
The years of stone are twenty-four; this hill of stone,
a skeleton to guard a yard of bone,
thrown by the windy guns of men together,
aspires to no heaven but the hill.

Ictinus built it; Pentelic marble brought
by the wealth of ships;
upraised, the columns breathed
in curves of marble.
Now bones breathe thinly in the yellow sun.
The architectures strive.

Beyond the city now to guard the hill
enormous guns and wealth
from the Baltic Sea to the Red
and through the Pacific to the Asian coast
as Romans stood
four hundred years along the Danube River

to guard both granaries and temples.

THE LONE RANGER

Vast unmapped badlands spread without a road.
No farmer drove tame oxen, ploughing loam
To seed his acreage; no settler's horse
But one time blundered riderless back home

While turkey buzzards gathered in the air
To make a circling tombstone. As for the law,
Sheriffs survived only if they could beat
Their images in mirrors to the draw.

Therefore he galloped on his silver horse:
He stood for law and order. Anarchy
Like flood or fire roared through every pass
But he and Tonto hid behind a tree

And when the bandits met to split the loot
He blocked the door. With silver guns he shot
The quick six-shooters from their snatching hands
And took them off to jail and let them rot.

For him the badlands were his mother's face.
He made an order where all order lacked,
From Hanged Boy Junction to the Rio Grande.
Why did he wear a mask? He was abstract.

A FRIEND REVISITED

Beside the door
She stood whom I had known before.
I saw the work of seven years
In graying hair and worried eyes,
And in a smile:
"Find in me only what appears,
And let me rest a while."

Though it had not been honesty
Always to say the sudden word

When she was young,
I liked the old disguise
Better than what I heard —
False laughter on the tongue
That once had made all efforts to seem free.

I do not ask for final honesty,
Since none can say,
"This is my motive, this is me,"
But I will pray
Deliberation and a shaping choice
To make a speaking voice.

ELEGY FOR WESLEY WELLS

Against the clapboards and the window panes
The loud March whines with rain and heavy wind,
In dark New Hampshire where his widow wakes.
She cannot sleep. The familiar length is gone.
I think across the clamorous Atlantic
To where the farm lies hard against the foot
Of Ragged Mountain, underneath Kearsarge.
The storm and hooded wind of equinox
Contend against New England's bolted door
Across the sea and set the signals out
Eastport to Block Island.
I speak his name against the beating sea.

The farmer dead, his horse will run to fat,
Go stiff and lame and whinny from his stall.
His dogs will whimper through the webby barn,
Where spiders close his tools in a pale gauze
And wait for flies. The nervous woodchuck now

Will waddle plumply through the garden weeds,
Eating wild peas as if he owned the land,
And the fat hedgehog pick the apple trees.
When next October's frosts harden the ground
And fasten in the year's catastrophe,
The farm will come undone —
The farmer dead, and deep in his ploughed earth.

Before the Civil War the land was used,
And railroads came to all the villages;
Before the war, a man with land was rich;
He cleared a dozen or two dozen acres,
Burning the timber, stacking up the stones,
And cultivated all his acreage
And planted it to vegetables to sell.
But then the war took off the hired men;
The fields grew up, to weeds and bushes first,
And then the fields were thick with ashy pine.
The faces of prosperity and luck
Turned westward with the railroads from New England.
Poverty settled, and the first went off,
Leaving their fathers' forty-acre farms,
To Manchester and Nashua and Lowell,
And traded the Lyceum for the block.
Now the white houses fell, among the wars,
From eighteen-sixty-five, for eighty years,
The Georgian firmness sagged, and the paint chipped,
And the white houses rotted to the ground.
Great growths of timber felled grew up again
On what had once been cultivated land,
On lawns and meadows, and from cellarholes.
Deep in the forest now, half covered up,
The reddened track of an abandoned railroad
Heaved in the frosts, in roots of the tall pines;
A locomotive stood
Like a strange rock, red as the fallen needles.

The farmer worked from four and milking time
To nine o'clock and shutting up the hens.
The heavy winter fattened him: the spring
Required his work and left his muscles lame.
By nineteen-forty, only the timid young
Remained to plough or sell.
He was the noble man in the sick place.

I number out the virtues that are dead,
Remembering the soft consistent voice
And bone that showed in each deliberate word.
I walk along old England's crowded shore
Where storm has driven everyone inside.
Soon I will leave, to cross the hilly sea
And walk again among familiar hills
In dark New Hampshire where his widow wakes.
The length of Wesley Wells, old man I loved,
Today was carried to the lettered plain
In Andover
While March bent down the cemetery trees.

1954–1958

———————

MY SON MY EXECUTIONER

My son, my executioner,
  I take you in my arms,
Quiet and small and just astir
  And whom my body warms.

Sweet death, small son, our instrument
  Of immortality,
Your cries and hungers document
  Our bodily decay.

We twenty-five and twenty-two,
  Who seemed to live forever,
Observe enduring life in you
  And start to die together.

CONDUCT AND WORK

1 *The Question*
Mirror, mirror on the wall,
Who is Donald Andrew Hall?

2
I am no Faust: unsalaried my sin;
It is from love I ask the devil in.

3
When that sweet action is at last unloosed,
How can you tell seducer from seduced?

Even the dignity of Christ
Whose churches were clean white
Here sinks.
The sixty-mile-an-hour tourist thinks
How quaint the rack
And ruin which attack
The limbs of Christ,
The Christian light.
Where once a hundred farmers came to pray,
Today twelve relicts sit
While a fatigued young man can say his bit.
The high blue air of August stands today
Over the heavy hay,
Whose facets now the small winds multiply.
But the dead houses cannot take the hay.
The cellarholes that populate the hills,
And the abandoned farms the roads pass by,
Only the spider fills.
The tall hay slopes to the earth uncut;
The doors of the old Grange are shut
And paint flakes from its clapboard wall:
The labor and the land together fall.
The rush of cars
Is all the noise that jars
Immobile earth, unbroken, thin, and old.
A crowd of pines and maples spreads along
Acres of ancient garden gone to wood,
And where a farmhouse stood,
There is a sign of something wrong —
A maple touched in part by blight or cold
So that one branch is red, on a green tree.
Death of a part is agony;
So far one branch is red on this green tree.

CHRISTMAS EVE IN WHITNEYVILLE

December, and the closing of the year;
The momentary carolers complete
Their Christmas Eves, and quickly disappear
Into their houses on each lighted street.

Each car is put away in each garage;
Each husband home from work, to celebrate,
Has closed his house around him like a cage,
And wedged the tree until the tree stood straight.

Tonight you lie in Whitneyville again,
Near where you lived, and near the woods or farms
Which Eli Whitney settled with the men
Who worked at mass-producing firearms.

The main street, which was nothing after all
Except a school, a stable, and two stores,
Was improvised and individual,
Picking its way alone, among the wars.

Now Whitneyville is like the other places,
Ranch houses stretching flat beyond the square,
Same stores and movie, same composite faces
Speaking the language of the public air.

Old houses of brown shingle still surround
This graveyard where you wept when you were ten
And helped to set a coffin in the ground.
You left a friend from school behind you then,

And now return, a man of fifty-two.
Talk to the boy. Tell him about the years
When Whitneyville quadrupled, and how you
And all his friends went on to make careers,

Had cars as long as hayracks, boarded planes
For Rome or Paris where the pace was slow
And took the time to think how yearly gains,
Profit and volume made the business grow.

"The things I had to miss," you said last week,
"Or thought I had to, take my breath away."
You propped yourself on pillows, where your cheek
Was hollow, stubbled lightly with new gray.

This love is jail; another sets us free.
Tonight the houses and their noise distort
The thin rewards of solidarity.
The houses lean together for support.

The noises fail, and lights go on upstairs.
The men and women are undressing now
To go to sleep. They put their clothes on chairs
To take them up again. I think of how,

All over Whitneyville, when midnight comes,
They lie together and are quieted,
To sleep as children sleep, who suck their thumbs,
Cramped in the narrow rumple of each bed.

They will not have unpleasant thoughts tonight.
They make their houses jails, and they will take
No risk of freedom for the appetite,
Or knowledge of it, when they are awake.

The lights go out and it is Christmas Day.
The stones are white, the grass is black and deep.
I will go back and leave you here to stay
Where the dark houses harden into sleep.

THE HOLE

He could remember that in the past, seven months ago,
and much of the time for fifty years before that,
his body walked without pain. He breathed in and out
without knowing that he was breathing, and he woke up
each day to the day's process
as if it were nothing to wake and dress in the morning.

When the doctor confided that his body would flake away
like a statue of rust, he looked into the long mirror
at his own strong shoulders with the skin smooth over them
and at his leg muscles which continued to be firm.
He announced to his body,
"We have resolved, and we will hold to our purpose."

Then eyes faded, limbs dwindled, skin puckered, lungs filled.
He dug himself into the private hole of his dying
and when he talked to his wife his voice came from a distance
as if he had married his pain, and lived alone with her.
He kept himself cold
and lay and twisted and slept, until nobody called him.

COPS AND ROBBERS

When I go West you wear a marshal's star,
    Persistent as a curse;
    And when I steal a purse
A note inside says, "I know who you are."

In England I am awfully on my guard.
    With a new mustache I live

In Soho as a spiv
Until you drop around from Scotland Yard.

In Paris with a black beret I sell
    Disgusting pictures to
    Americans; but you
Appear disguised among my clientèle.

In far Antarctica with Admiral Byrd
    I feel secure, though chilly,
    Till toward me with a billy
An outsize penguin lumbers from the herd.

THE SLEEPING GIANT

a hill in Connecticut

The whole day long, under the walking sun
That poised an eye on me from its high floor,
Holding my toy beside the clapboard house
I looked for him, the summer I was four.

I was afraid the waking arm would break
From the loose earth and rub against his eyes
A fist of trees, and the whole country tremble
In the exultant labor of his rise;

Then he with giant steps in the small streets
Would stagger, cutting off the sky, to seize
The roofs from house and home because we had
Covered his shape with dirt and planted trees;

And then kneel down and rip with fingernails
A trench to pour the enemy Atlantic

Into our basin, and the water rush,
With the streets full and all the voices frantic.

That was the summer I expected him.
Later the high and watchful sun instead
Walked low behind the house, and school began,
And winter pulled a sheet over his head.

DANCERS

Bowing he asks her the favor;
 Blushing she answers she will;
Waltzing they turn through the ballroom
  Swift in their skill.

Blinder than buffers of autumn,
 Deaf but to music's delight,
They dance like the puppets of music
  All through the night.

Out of the ball they come dancing
 And into the marketing day,
Waltzing through ignorant traffic,
  Bound to be gay.

They slacken and stoop, they are tired,
 They walk in a weather of pain;
Now wrinkles dig into their faces,
  Harsh as the rain.

They walk by identical houses
 And enter the one that they know.
They are old, and their children like houses
  Stand in a row.

No Deposit   No Return
  Said the bottle dead of beer.
Toughly by small things we learn
  Courage in this hemisphere,
Bleak and honest to affirm
A single independent term.

It only hurts me when I laugh,
  Said the hunter crucified:
I'm not Jesus Christ by half,
  So keep all weapons from my side
Or you'll take a dead man's curse;
Life is hell but death is worse.

In the caves of the Dordogne
  Paleolithic doctors made
Records with their flint and stone
  Of the slogans of the trade:
Strike the big bulls in the heart;
Leave the pregnant cows apart.

Shoot these old gray hairs, she said,
  But spare your country's flag! He thought —
Then Stonewall Jackson went ahead
  And ordered Barbara Frietchie shot.
His loyal soldiers cheered to see   ,
This total lack of chivalry.

The hairy fetch of felt disease,
  Which glories in its brutal name,
Eats anguish like a Stilton cheese
  And spreads in process crafty blame,
Until no person fouled by it
Can keep the savors separate.

Dillinger the killer died
  In a theater lobby when
One who slept at his own side
  Squealed his name to the G-men.
His final utterance was heard
To be a single nasty word.

Though the name of failure bray
  Like a donkey in despair,
Who must weep that jacks betray
  In the dark the darling mare,
We shall take our failures up
And drink them down from the full cup.

It only hurts us when we bray,
  Paleolithic G-men sighed.
Disease is hairier today,
  Said Barbara Frietchie crucified.
Then she added, from the hearse,
Life is hell but death is worse.

Dillinger spoke, and doctors drew
  Records of what the killer said,
Where Stonewall Jackson came to view
  Six pregnant cows untimely dead,
Upon whose sides one could discern
No Deposit   No Return

THE BODY POLITIC

I shot my friend to save my country's life.
After the happy bullet struck him dead,
I was saluted by the drum and fife
Corps of a high school, while the traitor bled.

27

I understood the duty they assigned
And shot my friend to save my sanity:
Keeping disorder from the state of mind
Was mental hygiene, as it seemed to me.

I never thought until I pulled the trigger
But that I did the difficult and good:
I thought republics stood for something bigger,
For the mind of man, as Plato said they stood.

Correct in politics, I felt depressed.
How could this be? Guilty, I walked to where
My orders issued from, or so I guessed.
Nothing was there, nothing, nothing but air.

Talkative Socrates committed treason
Against instinct and natural emotion
By drinking hemlock on behalf of reason.
Too late I learn: A nation's just a notion.

A SECOND STANZA

I put my hat upon my head
And walk'd into the Strand;
And there I met another man
Whose hat was in his hand.

The only trouble with the man
Whom I had met was that,
As he walked swinging both his arms,
His head was in his hat.

TO THE LOUD WIND

Mime the loud wind in pain —
The worded room will yield
Your canny agony
Not excellence nor will.

Dreams and asylums build
No words of sounding luck.
The metronome of guilt
Does sums behind the lock.

A maiden intellect
Sits safe indoors and still
When loud complexity
Thunders electrical.

Not subtlety nor guilt
But will made concentrate
Shouts the loud wind to fill
The worded intellect.

ABROAD THOUGHTS FROM HOME

My history extends
Where moved my tourist hands,
Who traveled on their own
Without a helping brain.

My hands that domineered
My body lacking mind
Pulled me around the globe
Like any country rube.

No more automaton,
Smarter and settled down,
I choose to move my hands
Which way my will extends.

I marvel now to mark
The geographic work
Done by my brainless touch
On every foreign latch.

In active consciousness
I now rehearse those trips
Which I no longer take
And only partly took.

FATHERS AND SONS

Over my bed
  My father stood,
Fixed in the stead
  Of abstract God.

I swore to build
  A place of play

Without a willed
  Authority.

Today I stand
  Above a son,
Though I had planned
  Catch as catch can.

Over my bed
  Last night there stood
The form I dread
  Of father God.

A SMALL FIG TREE

I am dead, to be sure,
for thwarting Christ's pleasure,
Jesus Christ called Saviour.

I was a small fig tree.
Unjust it seems to me
that I should withered be.

If justice sits with God,
Christ is cruel Herod
and I by magic dead.

If there is no justice
where great Jehovah is,
I will the devil kiss.

JE SUIS UNE TABLE

It has happened suddenly,
by surprise, in an arbor,
or while drinking good coffee,
after speaking, or before,

that I dumbly inhabit
a density; in language,
there is nothing to stop it,
for nothing retains an edge.

Simple ignorance presents,
later, words for a function,
but it is common pretense
of speech, by a convention,

and there is nothing at all
but inner silence, nothing
to relieve on principle
now this intense thickening.

SHUDDER

The foot of death has printed on my chest
Its signature, and I am rattled free
Of time and its dimensions and the rest
Of the hard outlines of identity.
Now minutes mix with centuries as if
Time were an undeciphered hieroglyph;
  For someone has walked on my grave.

O someone, walk in other places, please,
Whoever, when, or where your self may be,
That I may deal with near anxieties,
In fear of now and not eternity,
That future where you wander without guilt
Over the grass my private body built;
    For someone has walked on my grave.

"Grandfather Fool, thin voice I sometimes hear
Like scratches on a crystal radio,
Nothing I do will make death disappear
Or let your shudder or your knowledge go.
See the world whole, and see it clearly then,
A globe of dirt crusted with bones of men.
    If we walk, we walk on graves."

BY THE EXETER RIVER

"What is it you're mumbling, old Father, my Dad?
Come drink up your soup and I'll put you to bed."

"By the Exeter River, by the river, I said."

"Stop dreaming of rivers, old Father, my Dad,
Or save all your dreaming till you're tucked in bed."

"It was cold by the river. We came in a sled."

"It's colder to think of, old Father, my Dad,
Than blankets and bolsters and pillows of bed."

"We took off his dress and the cap from his head."

"Outside? In the winter? Old Father, my Dad,
What can you be thinking? Let's get off to bed."

"And Sally, poor Sally I reckon is dead."

"Was she your old sweetheart, old Father, my Dad?
Now lean on my shoulder and come up to bed."

"We drowned the baby. I remember we did."

THE UMBRELLA

It keeps out everything! It goes
Down to the floor, takes root and grows,
Until it is a wooden thing
Protecting me from wind and rain
So that no element constrain
My random perfect tarrying.
It is a game of solitaire.
Like water ouzels, I protect
My body in a case of air
While walking on the world, suspect
To all the trout for whom I seem
A foreign object in the stream.
I read in here. I see your lips
That move to answer me, but I
Am deaf to everyone's reply.
I am my own acquaintanceships.
The world is made of Indians
Whose bows and arrows have no sense.
I live in no man's land, it's true,

But in a Sherman tank for you
To shoot at if you care to shoot.
My armor plate is absolute.
Life does not scrape against my skin,
And wail, and struggle to get in.
I sacrificed my own design
To make this big umbrella mine.
I sleep much better now. The air
Is not conditioned but ignored,
Somehow as if I could afford
To breathe aromas of nowhere.
That's where I live. You hear me shout.
You see my inner happiness.
Your lips move. You are all a mess.
You will not get me to come out.

THE HUT OF THE MAN ALONE

Jerome had lived alone for thirty years.
Last winter, hunting in a freezing spell,
We found him huddled frozen at his well,
Bent double on the rocky lip of it,
As if he stared for something through the tears
That hardened on his beard and looked like sweat.

We took him home. What was it that we sensed?
I hacked the lock to open the black hut
The man alone had managed to keep shut.
I felt, of course, like some damned interferer.
The winter sun bent in, and caught against
The shattered pieces of a wall of mirror.

We live by love, but not by love alone,
He said, and I am subject like the rest.
Sometimes I meet an oyster which has grown
To the world's bulk, which sucks into its chest
Everything that I own
In its
World-love, the organ of
Encirclement. Oysters are jails. Half-wits
And frightened people too afraid to move
Drown in an oyster's keep. When Jane admits
Her love is cosmic, Phil has lost her love.

The thing, he said, is to discriminate
Inside a space, yet make discrimination
No politics to prettify the hate
Toward what invades an isolated nation;
Never to reach the state
Of Ted,
The clever eremite,
Whose cave has comforts like a single bed,
Books, records, pictures, and a reading light;
He cons himself; the text is in his head.
"Who's worth the time?" said Annie. She was right.

Take in with the right hand, he said; put off with the left.
Speak and then speak. Let both hands learn to speak,
For if one hand should come to be more deft,
The other hand and talent would be weak;
The poise must always shift.
"Too late,"
A sane man called "the two
Unendurable words. Wastage of life will create
The implication of death," which means that you

Must tell your love while you reveal your hate,
And never leave your hands nothing to do.

1934

In nineteen-thirty-four we spent July
At a small farm, my mother's father's. I
Was five years old. Father got *White's News-Letter*,
Fridays, which said that things were looking better.
Bright Model A's kept speeding past each day,
Fouled by the eagles of the N.R.A.,
And blew their brassy horns at us, the farm
Where nothing and no one ever came to harm.
Men walked along the ditch, alone or in twos,
Stopping to let the sand out of their shoes,
And saw the house stretch back, a decent wall
Of clapboard, like a house they could recall.
They always stopped. My father said they might
Burn us and all the cattle up at night
If we refused them food. Grandmother spread
The butter that she churned upon the bread
The baker peddled, airy, corrupt, and stale,
And dipped them milk, out of my grandfather's pail,
And answered that we had no work right here,
Leastwise right now, but maybe they could peer
Up north a ways, perhaps and possibly.
At any rate, she knew that she could see
Pine timber trucking south in a heavy load
Five or six times a day. They took the road
Up north, or hopped a freight at Danbury where
Freight stopped to give the mail a thoroughfare.
Who needed mail in nineteen-thirty-four?
Somebody did, who needed it before.

Glass, air, ice, light,
and winter cold.
They stand on all the corners,
waiting alone, or in
groups that talk like the air
moving branches. It
is Christmas, and a red dummy
laughs in the window
of a store. Although
the trolleys come,
no one boards them,
but everyone moves
up and down, stamping his feet,
so unemployed.
They are talking, each of them,
but it is sticks and stones
that hear them,
their plans,
exultations,
and memories of the old time.
The words fly out, over
the roads and onto
the big, idle farms, on the hills,
forests, and rivers
of America, to mix into silence
of glass, air, ice, light,
and winter cold.

THE THREE MOVEMENTS

It is not in the books
that he is looking, nor for
a new book, nor
documents of any kind, nor
does he expect it to be like the wind,
that, when you touch it, tears
without a sound of tearing, nor
like the rain
water
that becomes
grass in the sun. He
expects that when he finds it,
it will be
like a man, visible, alive
to what has happened and what
will happen, with
firmness in its face, seeing
exactly what is, without
measure of change, and not
like documents,
or rain in the grass.

But what, he says,
if it is not
for the finding, not
what you most expect, nor even
what you dread, nothing
but the books, the endless
documents, the banked
volumes that repeat
mile after mile
their names,
their information?

Perhaps there is nothing
except the rain
water
becoming the grass, the
sustenance. What
a man should do is
accumulate
information
until he has gathered, like a
farmer, as much
as his resources can contain.

Yet perhaps, he thinks,
I speak
with knowledge, but perhaps
forgetting the movement
that intrigues
all thinking. It is
the movement which works through,
which discovers itself
in alleys, in
sleep, not
expected and not
in the books of words and phrases
nor the various paints and edges
of scenery.
It is, he says,
familiar when come upon,
glimpsed
as in a mirror
unpredicted,
and it appears
to understand. It is
like himself, only visible.

SESTINA

Hang it all, Ezra Pound, there is only the one sestina,
Or so I thought before, always supposing
The subject of them invariably themselves.
That is not true. Perhaps they are nearly a circle,
And they tell their motifs like party conversation,
Formally repetitious, wilfully dull,

But who are we to call recurrence dull?
It is not exact recurrence that makes a sestina,
But a compromise between a conversation
And absolute repetition. It comes from supposing
That there is a meaning to the almost-circle,
And that laws of proportion speak of more than themselves.

I think of the types of men who have loved themselves,
Who studious of their faces made them dull
To find them subtle; for the nearly-a-circle,
This is the danger. The introvert sestina
May lose its voice by childishly supposing
It holds a hearer with self-conversation.

When we are bound to a tedious conversation,
We pay attention to the words themselves
Until they lose their sense, perhaps supposing
Such nonsense is at very least less dull.
Yet if the tongue is held by a sestina,
It affirms not words but the shape of the unclosed circle.

The analogy: not the precise circle,
Nor the loose patching of a conversation
Describes the repetition of a sestina;
Predictable, yet not repeating themselves
Exactly, they are like life, and hardly dull,
And not destroyed by critical supposing.

Since there is nothing precise (always supposing)
Consider the spiraling, circular, not full-circle
As the type of existence, the dull and never dull,
Predictable, general movement of conversation,
Where things seem often more, slightly, than themselves,
And make us wait for the coming, like a sestina.

And so we name the sestina's subject, supposing
Our lives themselves dwindle, an incomplete circle;
About which, conversation is not dull.

A SET OF SEASONS

He suspects that the seasons
Are not as they should be. How
Should he know that seasons
Are not to be suspected?

This gelatin of air
And splendid haze infers
Mistaken complements
To circumstance and phrase.

How should he come to know?
And how to score the seasons,
When he is making them
As red as grass, backwards?

Sir, the beginnings of pleasure
Erupt from the green and the red,
Scored in the head as grass,
Seasonal, unsuspected.

"THE SCREAM"

Observe. Ridged, raised, tactile, the horror
of the skinned head is there. It is skinned
which had a covering-up before,
and now is nude, and is determined

by what it perceives. The blood not Christ's,
blood of death without resurrection,
winds flatly in the air. Habit foists
conventional surrender to one

response in vision, but it fails here,
where the partaking viewer is freed
into the under-skin of his fear.
Existence is laid bare, and married

to a movement of caught perception
where the unknown will become the known
as one piece of the rolling mountain
becomes another beneath the stone

which shifts now toward the happy valley
which is not prepared, as it could not
be, for the achieved catastrophe
which produces no moral upshot,

no curtain, epilogue, nor applause,
no Dame to return purged to the Manse
(the Manse is wrecked) — not even the pause,
the repose of art that has distance.

"MARAT'S DEATH"

Charlotte, "the angel of assass-
ination," is unrelaxed.
She is not deep but she is tall.

Marat is dead. The people
of France will endure his death,
l'ami du peuple and no man.

Charlotte, the will begins to
revise you to leather. How
volition hurts the skin of girls!

Marat had skin which boiled like
water on a stove. His wet
and cruel skin has one wound more.

Charlotte is standing naked
and simple above the bed.
Her body is an alphabet.

"THE KISS"

The backs twist with the kiss
and the mouth which is the hurt
and the green depth of it
holds plainly the hour.

The aim loses its lie.
We are victims, and we shift

in the cloyed wind, the dark
harm. No, in the thick

of rubbed numbness, and we
are the winter of the air,
and the not-nothing, blurred,
bound, motion declared.

At night, wound in the clothes
of the groomed and unendured,
where the five hands of wire
rasp, hurt me, and fold,

we love. Love is a kiss
which adheres like the feet
of a green lizard to walls
whole days, and is gone.

"BETWEEN THE CLOCK AND THE BED"

In the yellow light, an old man
stands between the clock and the bed.
While he paints the picture, this old
painter lives among clock and bed
as if three elderly brothers
still inhabited the house where
they were born. But the grandfather's
clock annoys the painter; it keeps on
measuring its pendulum back
and forth, insistent, repeating
itself as if he heard nothing.

He becomes angry, and decides
to shut the clock up. He thinks: What
can I use, in this furnished room?
He remembers putting a gun
among his linen handkerchiefs
but when he looks, it is not there.
Perhaps it is in the locker
by the wall. He kneels beside it
but the clasps are too difficult.
He feels extremely tired. He crawls
up to the narrow bed, and sleeps
in the clock's light which is yellow.

CHRIST CHURCH MEADOWS

Often I saw, as on my balcony
    I stirred the afternoon into my tea,
Enameled swards descending to the *Thames*,
    Called *Isis* here, and flowers that were gems,
Cattle in herds, and great senescent trees,
    Through which, as Pope predicted, ran the breeze.
Ad sinistram, where limpid *Cherwell* flows,
    Often I saw the punts of gallant beaux
Who sang like shepherds to each gentle love
    Quaint tales of Trojan warriors to prove
That loving Maidens are rewarded here
    With bastards and with pints of watered beer.
Here too I saw my countrymen at large,
    Expending *Kodachrome* upon a barge.
From chauffered *Car*, or touring *Omnibus*,
    They leered at me, calling me "them," not "us."
A jutting woman came to me and said,
    "Your *Highness*, can those big white geese be fed?"

46

"*Yankee* go home," I snarled. "Of course the *Swans,*
   As the *Bard* puts it, are reserved for *Dons.*"
She fainted then, beside two *Christ Church* porters,
   Who cast her, as I told them, on the waters.

THE CLOWN

"Practically all you newspaper people,"
the Clown said, "get it badly mixed up
with sentimental junk, but you are a chap

"with an intelligent face. I am not crying
on the inside. I am no brave faker.
On the contrary, I am a simple laugh,

"and the laugh pretends to be about
nothing in particular, and not the answer
to anyone's especially difficult question.

"Nor do I pretend that the world is really,
in its deep center, utterly pleasant,
or lovely as a joke, or that it feels good

"to be crucified. Laughter is the sign
of an emotion that is like other emotions
but more transient and less related

"to the problems of the man who displays it.
It is my specialty, and all laughs
are mad laughs. I realize that I could argue

"that these red polka dots are spots
of blood, and that I laugh to explain them,
but any reason is a false reason;

"polka dots are as crazy as polka dots,
or as the light heart itself,
which suddenly laughs in the shuttered room

"that is real and unhappy, where the old
without chances talk to the young without hope.
Men dying of cancer, even,

"lift for a second in their hollow bodies
no hope, but a lightness like air.
They don't stay lifted. (What will stay lifted?)

"If even for men dying, there is my madness,
who puts me out of work?" The Clown
cartwheeled across the dressing room, and bowed.

PRESIDENT AND POET

Granted that what we summon is absurd:
Mustaches and the stick, the New York fake
In cowboy costume grinning for the sake
Of cameras that always just occurred;
Granted that his Rough Riders fought a third-
Rate army badly general'd, to make
Headlines for Mr. Hearst; that one can take
Trust-busting not exactly at its word:

Robinson, alcoholic and unread,
Received a letter with a White House frank.
To court the Muse, you'd think T.R.'d've killed her
And had her stuffed, and yet this mountebank
Chose to belaurel Robinson instead
Of famous men like Richard Watson Gilder.

48

RELIGIOUS ARTICLES

By the road to church, Shaker Village
glints with prosperity in an age
lacking Shakers. New signs hosannah:
RELIGIOUS ARTICLES RELIGIEUX,
and a new Ford waits to be drawn for,
in the Bishop's Fund, in November.

"I come to the garden alone," where
old women's voices strain and quiver
to the organ one of them has played
for sixty years. The house which was made
for the farm Sunday lacks a preacher.
Ten women, two old men, and I hear

a boy in the pulpit measure out
a brutal sermon. His sky-blue suit
took the diploma from high school just
two months ago. The watch on his wrist
his cousin gave him ticks the time he
must wait for college, cloth, and city.

Among the dead of this village church
the old women's voices use the pitch
of the pumping organ to lean on;
light comes through the trees and the dark green
curtains speckled with holes, and light hits
the frayed red cloth of the cushioned seats.

I stand among the relics of childhood
and the century before. My dead
crowd into the pew; I hear their thin
voices complain in a reedy hymn
of parch in the garden, of hunger
for rest, and of the words that I hear:

"We who do not exist make noises
only in you. Your illusion says
that we who are cheated and broken
croon our words to the living again.
You must not believe in anything;
you who feel cheated are crooning."

THE FOUNDATIONS
OF AMERICAN INDUSTRY

In the Ford plant
at Ypsilanti
men named for their
fathers work at steel
machines named Bliss,
Olaffson, Smith-Grieg,
and Safety.

In the Ford plant
the generators
move quickly on
belts, a thousand now
an hour. New men
move to the belt when
the shift comes.

For the most part
the men are young, and
go home to their
Fords, and drive around,
or watch TV,
sleep, and then go work,
toward payday;

when they walk home
they walk on sidewalks
marked W
P A 38;
their old men made
them, and they walk on
their fathers.

THE WIDOWS

Up and down the small streets, in which
no two houses are exactly
alike, widows of all ages
sit alone playing solitaire,
or knitting, or sometimes baking,
left in the big, empty houses.

Here are Mrs. Montgomery,
Mrs. Pilching, Mrs. Wolf, and
Mrs. Pelletier, all at once —
in a section of nine houses,
four widows. Sometimes they have bridge,
including either lunch or tea.

In the summer, separately,
widows spend a month in hotels
in New Hampshire, or sometimes Maine,
but never in Massachusetts.
In the winter, or some winters,
some of them go to Florida.

Book clubs, television, and ways
to supplement their small incomes

keep them busy. It is not a
bad life, they say, for there are so
many left like you, though no two
widows are exactly alike.

MR. AND MRS. BILLINGS

"Your wife," the doctor said,
"Will be dead
In approximately twelve weeks."
His left shoe creaks,
Thought Mr. Billings; and why does he look
Like a doctor in a book
Or a cigarette ad?
But Mr. Billings was sad
That his wife was dying.
Flying
To his neighborhood florist, he bought
More flowers than he ought,
And sent them to her;
Then wished they had been fewer
For fear she should understand
His motive, and
Ask questions. Then
Mr. Billings thought again,
Of how to make each
Moment reach
Beauty and pleasure beyond the expected.
A friend named Herbert Peck did,
With a success Mr. Billings thought a wonder,
As he remembered, under
Similar circumstances,
By taking his wife to dances,

Bingo, and the race track —
Things she had learned to lack.
Mr. Billings, on the other hand,
Quickly planned
A journey to France,
And took a chance
On a new Buick, and made
Arrangements for lemonade
To be delivered twice a day.
Now at rest, and almost gay,
Preparing for a visiting hour
When he must be a tower
Of reassurance, he sits
With a packet of Ritz
Crackers and a bottle of Coke,
To think of a suitable, and funny, joke.

THE FAMILY

Under the glassy Christmas tree,
the packages wait for Daddy
    who is asleep. He remembers,
gripping the sheet, some old story

in which he eats his own mother's
affable dog, yet is it hers
    or his, or his kids' dog, or his
kids themselves that he eats? Lovers

will remember the reverses
suffered in dreams. Now he stretches
    awake, and thinks, it is Christmas:
Gramps will come (without Flo, who is

the new wife, who goes to High Mass
with the kind of people she has
    known all her life), and Auntie, too,
with Roy and the kids, to trespass

their once-a-year. He wonders who
will be the first to get into
    the bourbon too far tonight. He
will manage to mention his due,

and Gramps will threaten him (greedy
as Flo is!), saying, "Oh, there'll be
    a surprise or two, I warrant."
He will remind Roy that the three

hundred still asks for repayment
(that Roy had promised would be sent
    him in nineteen-forty-seven).
Each kid will look at each parent

for a while, and go out (listen
to their motorcycles!) and then
    return to sit in a huddle,
also drunk. He looks to straighten

his tie, now, and descends to fill
his stomach with oat cereal.
    He is hungry, very hungry;
he thinks he could eat an animal.

THE GROWN-UPS

Lady, what are you laughing at? Is it the joke
that Harry is telling, about the Jew and the pork?
But you heard it from your Grampa the poultry salesman
when you were only four years old.

Mister, whose hand are you shaking? Name him.
You say you didn't catch the name?
Then why did you ask him to come to Canada
in August with you, Emily, and the kids?

Doctor, what is in your black bag? What is inside
the knobby machines in your office, Doctor?
Sugar and air, your black looks tell me,
sugar and air to cure their diseases.

Lawyer, your briefcase is snappy with papers.
Whose justice do you argue? Money's? Is that it?
Money, money, money —
I hear the lawyer and his clients praying.

Mother, you make your son afraid
of death, and your daughter afraid of her father.
Father, you come home from your office to your cellar
and pound nails into the skin of wood.

(I remember hearing their voices talk
downstairs, while I listened awake in my bed,
not understanding particular words, but the pitch
of the laughter, the lies, the responsive pitches.)

1959–1963

THE LONG RIVER

The musk ox smells
in his long head
my boat coming. When
I feel him there,
intent, heavy,

the oars make wings
in the white night,
and deep woods are close
on either side
where trees darken.

I rowed past towns
in their black sleep
to come here. I passed
the northern grass
and cold mountains.

The musk ox moves
when the boat stops,
in hard thickets. Now
the wood is dark
with old pleasures.

THE SNOW

Snow is in the oak.
Behind the thick, whitening
air which the wind drives,
the weight of the sun

presses the snow
on the pane of my window.

I remember snows and my walking
through their first fall in cities,
asleep or drunk
with the slow, desperate falling.
The snow blurs in my eyes
with other snows.

Snow is what must
come down, even if it struggles
to stay in the air with the strength
of the wind. Like an old man,
whatever I touch I turn
to the story of death.

Snow is what fills
the oak, and what covers
the grass and the bare garden.
Snow is what reverses
the sidewalk and the lawn
into the substance of whiteness.

So the watcher sleeps himself
back to the baby's eyes.
The tree, the breast, and the floor
are limbs of him, and from
his eyes he extends a skin
which grows over the world.

The baby is what must
have fallen, like snow. He resisted,
the way the old man
struggles inside the airy tent
to keep on breathing.
Birth is the fear of death.

Snow is what melts.
I cannot open the door
to the cycles of water.
The sun has withdrawn itself
and the snow keeps falling,
and something will always be falling.

THE FARM

Standing on top of the hay
in a good sweat,
I felt the wind from the lake
dry on my back,
where the chaff
grew like the down on my face.

At night on the bare boards
of the kitchen,
we stood while the old man
in his nightshirt gummed
the stale crusts
of his bread and milk.

Up on the gray hill
behind the barn, the stones
had fallen away
where the Penacook marked
a way to go
south from the narrow river.

By the side of the lake
my dead uncle's rowboat rots

in heavy bushes.
Slim pickerel glint
in the water. Black horned pout
doze on the bottom.

THE POEM

It discovers by night
what the day hid from it.
Sometimes it turns itself
into an animal.
In summer it takes long walks
by itself where meadows
fold back from ditches.
Once it stood still
in a quiet row of machines.
Who knows
what it is thinking?

THE TREE AND THE CLOUD

In the middle distance
a tree stands,
above it a cloud.

The tree is a raised fist.
It moves so slowly
you cannot see it move.

The cloud changes.
It is almost nothing,
and the wind pushes it.

The tree is an engine
for becoming itself
in the dirt and the sun.

The cloud resembles
whatever we see there.
The tree is chopped down

to be changed entirely,
but if the cloud rips
it becomes other clouds.

The tree is hard to the hands.
To touch the cloud
hardens the touching.

THE IDEA OF FLYING

The wings lacking a trunk
flap like a sail. Body
strains, follows, and stiffens the
meeting of grand jellies.

It weighs air. In the wind,
blank at the low margin,
high cuts in solids of
wind are the stone footsteps.

Unbent, loosed in the thick
sky and the walked heaven,
look, how the body of
space is a steep dying.

THE MOON

A woman who lived
in a tree caught
the moon in a kettle.

The wind on the roof
of the tree thumped
while she built her fire.

She boiled it down
to a flat bean
to set on her plate.

She swallowed the moon
and the moon grew
like a child inside her.

When the wind flew away
she mounted
the steps of the air

to bear the moon
on a dark bed
in the house of the night.

She nurses him
while the wind perches
like a heavy bird

in the void branches
of a tree, beside
a cold kettle.

THE SUN

He waited in the sadness of the sun's intention
with a toy in his hand. In cloudy weather or rain
or when the light turned to China he kept to himself
his own darkness. In the sun he knew he was followed.

THE CHILD

He lives among a dog,
a tricycle, and a friend.
Nobody owns him.

He walks by himself, beside
the black pool, in the cave
where icicles of rock

rain hard water,
and the walls are rough
with the light of stone.

He hears low talking
without words.
The hand of a wind touches him.

He walks until he is tired
or somebody calls him.
He leaves right away.

When he plays with his friend
he stops suddenly
to hear the black water.

THE KILL

Sheep move on the grass,
so rarely one imagines
small boulders.

Then a dog hurtles
into the field, like water.

The sheep flutter.
The dog tears among them
for five minutes. Then he diminishes

like a wind or a flood
into the rubble of distance.

THE SEA

I remember watching
from the porch of a cottage.
The loose bulk swayed.

. . .

She is the mother of calms
and the hot grasses;
the mother of cliffs
and of the grinding sand;
she is the mother of the dead
submarine, which rolls
on a beach among gulls.

. . .

The drunken waves argue
the same sentences
over and over, as if
no one will understand them.

WELLS

I lived in a dry well
under the rank grass of a meadow.

A white ladder leaned out of it
but I was afraid of the sounds

of animals grazing.
I crouched by the wall ten years

until the circle of a woman's darkness
moved over mine like a mouth.

The ladder broke out in leaves
and fruit hung from the branches.

I climbed to the meadow grass.
I drink from the well of cattle.

THE WRECKAGE

At the edge of the city the pickerel
vomits and dies. The river
with its white hair staggers to the sea.

My life lay crumpled like a smashed car.

Windows barred, ivy, square stone.
Lines gather at mouth and at eyes
like cracks in a membrane.
Eyeballs and tongue spill on the floor
in a puddle of yolks and whites.

The intact 707
under the clear wave, the sun shining.

The playhouse of my grandfather's mother
stands north of the shed: spiders
and the dolls' teacups of dead women.
In Ohio the K Mart shrugs;
it knows it is going to die.

A stone, the closed eye of the dirt.

Outside before dawn
houses sail up
like wrecks from the bottom of the sea.
A door clicks; a light opens.

If the world is a dream,
so is the puffed stomach of Juan,
and the rich in Connecticut are dreamers.

There are bachelors
who live in shacks made of oil cans
and broken doors, who stitch their shirts
until the cloth disappears under stitches,
who collect nails in Ball jars.

A trolley car comes out of the elms,
the tracks laid through an acre of wheat stubble,
slanting downhill. I board it,
and cross the field into the new pine.

AN AIRSTRIP IN ESSEX 1960

It is a lost road into the air.
It is a desert
among sugar beets.
The tiny wings
of the Spitfires of nineteen-forty-one
flake in the mud of the Channel.

Near the road a brick pillbox
totters under a load of grass,
where Home Guards waited
in the white fogs of the invasion winter.

Good night, old ruined war.

In Poland the wind rides on a jagged wall.
Smoke rises from the stones; no, it is mist.

NEW HAMPSHIRE

A bear sleeps in a cellarhole; pine needles
heap over a granite doorstep; a well brims
with acorns and the broken leaves of an oak
which grew where an anvil rusted in a forge.

Inside an anvil, inside a bear, inside a leaf,
a bark of rust grows on the tree of a gas pump;
EAT signs gather like leaves in the shallow
cellars of diners; a wildcat waits for deer

on the roof of a car. Blacktop buckled by frost
starts goldenrod from the highway. Fat honey bees
meander among raspberries, where a quarrel
of vines crawls into the spilled body of a plane.

SOUTHWEST OF BUFFALO

The long lakes, flanked
by the conservative
farms, which are asleep
but thinking, collect

water from the quiet
hills, which as they slope
and touch, make towns
to hide from the wind.
Near Ellington, in the Randolph
graveyard, Albert Gallatin Dow,
who died a hundred years old
in nineteen-eight,
remains in the granite tomb
which he ordered built
toward the day when the short beard
of even a centenarian
would blow in the wind
of flowers, on
the hills of New York.

SELF-PORTRAIT AS A BEAR

Here is a fat animal, a bear
that is partly a dodo.
Ridiculous wings hang at his shoulders
as if they were collarbones
while he plods in the bad brickyards
at the edge of the city, smiling
and eating flowers. He eats them
because he loves them
because they are beautiful
because they love him.
It is eating flowers which makes him so fat.
He carries his huge stomach
over the gutters of damp leaves
in the parking lots in October,
but inside that paunch

he knows there are fields of lupine
and meadows of mustard and poppy.
He encloses sunshine.
Winds bend the flowers
in combers across the valley,
birds hang on the stiff wind,
at night there are showers, and the sun
lifts through a haze every morning
of the summer in the stomach.

MYCENAE

In the shaft graves, butterflies
of gold flutter at the gold
masks of the Cretan traders.

Over the gate, the simple
lions of the Achaeans
stand upright in old combat.

The King climbed the long carpet
to be struck like a zebra
drinking at a water-hole.

ON A HORSE CARVED IN WOOD

The horses of the sea; remember
how the sea paws at its moving floor,
charging and failing. The mane on his

neck arched exactly in strength matches
the tail at the bend of waves breaking
on opposite shores. He is the king
of the wild waves, charging and failing.
When Master Zeus struck from the North, he
drove Poseidon the Horse to the sea.
Sacred to Poseidon are both the
nimble dolphin and the stiff pine tree.

JEALOUS LOVERS

When he lies in the night away from her,
the backs of his eyelids burn.
He turns in the darkness as if it were an oven.
The flesh parches and he lies awake
thinking of everything wrong.

In the morning when he goes to meet her,
his heart struggles at his ribs
like an animal trapped in its burrow.
Then he sees her running to meet him,
red-faced with hurry and cold.

She stumbles over the snow.
Her knees above orange knee-socks
bob in a froth of the hems
of skirt and coat and petticoat.
Her eyes have not shut all night.

SLEEPING

The avenue rises toward a city of white marble.
I am not meeting anyone. The capitol is empty.
I enter the dome of sleep.

. . .

I was lying on the sofa to rest, to sleep
a few minutes, perhaps.
I felt my body sag into the hole of sleep.
All at once I was awake and frightened.
My own death was drifting near me
in the middle of life. The strong body
blurred and diminished into the dark waters.
The flesh floated away.

. . .

The shadow is a tight passage
that no one will be spared
who goes down
to the deep well.
In sleep, something remembers.
Three times since I woke
from the first sleep,
it has drunk that water.
Awake, it is still sleeping.

"INTERNAL AND EXTERNAL FORMS"

What the birds say
is colored. Shade

feels the thickness
shrubs make in a
July growth,

heavy brown thorns
for autumn, curled
horns in double
rows. Listening
the birds fly

down, in shade. Leaves
of darkness turn
inward, noises
curve inward, and
the seed talks.

"KING AND QUEEN"

As they grew older,
the land which had grown wheat
washed down the hill,
and the river
carried the land into the sea.

The priest with the horned
mask, who brought meat
from the altar,
turned into a bird
and flew among mountains.

The people of the markets,
who touched their heads to the ground,

changed into clumps of weed
among the gutters
of the bare hill.

The King and Queen rule
over the dark nation
of thrones. As slowly
as a river builds a delta,
they have become still.

"RECLINING FIGURE"

Then the knee of the wave
turned to stone.

By the cliff of her flank
I anchored,

in the darkness of harbors
laid-by.

DIGGING

One midnight, after a day when lilies
lift themselves out of the ground while you watch them,
and you come into the house at dark
your fingers grubby with digging, your eyes
vague with the pleasure of digging,

let a wind raised from the South
climb through your bedroom window, lift you in its arms
— you have become as small as a seed —
and carry you out of the house, over the black garden,
spinning and fluttering,

and drop you in cracked ground.
The dirt will be cool, rough to your clasped skin
like a man you have never known.
You will die into the ground
in a dead sleep, surrendered to water.

You will wake suffering
a widening pain in your side, a breach
gapped in your tight ribs
where a green shoot struggles to lift itself upwards
through the tomb of your dead flesh

to the sun, to the air of your garden
where you will blossom
in the shape of your own self, thoughtless
with flowers, speaking
to bees, in the language of green and yellow, white and red.

"O FLODDEN FIELD"

The learned King fought
like a fool, flanked
and outtricked, who hacked
in a corner of cousins
until the ten thousand
swords lay broken,

and the women walked
in their houses alone.

On a journey among horses,
the spirit of a man who died
only a week ago
is walking through heather
and forgets that its body
had seventy years.
Wild horses are singing,
and voices of the rocks.

The spirit from the boneyard
finds a new life, in the field
where the King's wound
built the blackness of Glasgow
and the smoke of the air.
The spirit, like a boy,
picks up from the heather
a whole sword.

COLD WATER

He steps around a gate of bushes
in the mess
and trickle of a dammed stream
and his shoe fills with cold water. He
enters the shade
of a thicket, a black pool,
a small circle of stunned drowsing air

under the birch which meets overhead
as if smoke

rose up and turned into leaves.
He stands on the roots of a maple
and imagines
dropping a line. His wrist jumps
with the pain of a live mouth hooked deep,

and he stares to watch where the lithe stripe
tears water.
Then it heaves on his hand: cold,
square-tailed, flecked, revenant flesh
of a brook trout.
The pine forests he walked through
darken and cool a dead farmer's brook.

He looks up to see the Penacook
returning,
standing among the birches
on the other side of the black pool.
The five elders
have come for him, he is young,
his naked body whitens with cold

in the snow, blisters in the bare sun;
the ice cuts
him, the thorns of blackberries:
He is ready for the mystery.
He follows them
over the speechless needles
of pines which are dead or born again.

THE OLD PILOT

He discovers himself on an old airfield.
He thinks he was there before,
but rain has washed out the lettering of a sign.
A single biplane, all struts and wires,
stands in the long grass and wildflowers.
He pulls himself into the narrow cockpit
although his muscles are stiff
and sits like an egg in a nest of canvas.
He sees that the machine gun has rusted.
The glass over the instruments
has broken, and the red arrows are gone
from his gas gauge and his altimeter.
When he looks up, his propeller is turning,
although no one was there to snap it.
He lets out the throttle. The engine catches
and the propeller spins into the wind.
He bumps over holes in the grass,
and he remembers to pull back on the stick.
He rises from the land in a high bounce
which gets higher, and suddenly he is flying again.
He feels the old fear, and rising over the fields
the old gratitude. In the distance, circling
in a beam of late sun like birds migrating,
there are the wings of a thousand biplanes.

BEAU OF THE DEAD

John Fleming walked in the house his cousin left him
and wanted the very tick of the old stopped clock.
He wanted nothing of his own past. He wanted

the hour of the day at which an heiress was born
or the portrait finished of a virtuous aunt;
the temperature and the weather, the exact
feel of it, the sound and the stillness from the street
and the park, and the slant on the walls of the light
of afternoons that had been. He learned to enter
the intimate centuries of walnut sideboards,
to drowse with mahogany chairs, and to endure
with old tables the spill of good wine. He listened
when the stilled voices of the scrutable past
spoke, faintly and fine, from a mirror where he saw
no shadow of himself — the glass mottled with age —
but the resemblance of invisible girls,
Victorian ringlets and Alexandra fringe,
primping before a man they would not have cared for,
the beau of the dead, the gallant of dead ladies.

A VILLAGE IN EAST ANGLIA

He walks out of the village. The road
    lowers into a hollow
        which villagers call
    the Borough, though it contains
only a farm, a stream where small boys
        go newting,

and four medieval town houses
    which drop plaster in the frosts
        of winter, and which
    a decade will dismantle.
Their second storeys jut like the brows
        of children.

The road climbs, and he looks back across
the Borough at the long Church
like a cathedral
with its weathered carved stone
over the planes of the red-tiled roofs.
Dominant,

the spire pierces seven times the height
of the beech tree. The village
gathered by the spire
pointed toward a destiny
which ordained the narrow proportions
which please him.

Yet inside the Church, he remembers,
the deathwatch beetle hollows
six-hundred-year-old
beams. The Vicar reconstructs
old music and Sarum liturgy
for twelve souls.

He wanders south of the Church, and sees
the derelict mill which heaves
among the barley
of a high field and raises
nude vanes which the industrious wind
cannot turn.

He walks toward it, on lanes through barley.
Its pitted red brick is dark
against the green hills
opening past the village.
In a century of poor gleanings
it crushed wheat

for everyone's dark loaf. Its wide cone
taught the proportions of use.

Its ruin appalls
only an eye which invents
a landscape which needs it. It is there
to be climbed.

In the complicated village street
to which he descends, a truck
delivers milled flour
to the baker in his shop.
The curved street is a continuous
delicate

pargeting, and beyond the resumed
almoners' house, gas pumps lean
from the imagined
plaster and timber. He hears
the Vicar teaching his old cello
to the son

of the Tory grocer in the room
at the back of the grocer's
under the low oak
beams with the ship's markings on them,
which ten years of winter without heat
would crumble.

He goes home and makes tea at a stove
in a house which will vanish.
If he spills water
from kettle onto cokestove
it hurtles together from all sides
at once.

LETTER TO AN ENGLISH POET

Your letter describes
      what you see from your window. You chose,
among the council
      houses and gray cities, to observe

a destroyed abbey
      whose stones you touch for their proportion,
the lines of a mind
      although the mind is dead. I write you

from an old attic
      where the green of maples like a storm
cuts off my winter
      prospect of square blocks of the same house.

Maples are the past,
      for the settlers liked a good shade tree.
On the older blocks,
      ugly frame houses like ours recall

the German merchants
      who left their country to avoid war.
Rural Michigan
      took them in. It is sentimental

to love their houses
      for being burly like them, and trees
too are evasions.
      In America, the past exists

in the library.
      It is not the wind on the old stone.
The wind blows in you
      like power, and the blades of the mill turn.

Unmeasured voices
 shed lies in their vying to utter
like leaves from maples.
 Yet the loose roads and the twelve seasons

allow us to move.
 It is what we like most in ourselves.
Most of your country
 envies our worst houses, and would sell

abbeys if they could
 to Americans who collect. Some
here try to construct
 a new abbey without architects

or an idea,
 except to represent the shapeless
shape of a nation.
 All of them scatter with the dry leaves.

But the best of us
 have resembled instead the raiding
millionaires; without
 history, we pillage history.

Although museums
 glass-in our inheritance, how else
shall we inherit?
 Without parents we adopt the world.

STUMP

1

Today they cut down the oak.
Strong men climbed with ropes
in the brittle tree.
The exhaust of a gasoline saw
was blue in the branches.

The oak had been dead a year.
I remember the great sails of its branches
rolling out green, a hundred and twenty feet up,
and acorns thick on the lawn.
Nine cities of squirrels lived in that tree.

Yet I was happy that it was coming down.
"Let it come down!" I kept saying to myself
with a joy that was strange to me.
Though the oak was the shade of old summers,
I loved the guttural saw.

2

By night a bare trunk stands up fifteen feet
and cords of firewood press
on the twiggy frozen grass of the yard.
One man works every afternoon for a week
to cut the trunk gradually down.

Bluish stains spread through the wood
and make it harder to cut.
He says they are the nails of a trapper
who dried his pelts on the oak
when badgers dug in the lawn.

Near the ground he hacks for two days,
knuckles scraping the stiff snow.

His chain saw breaks three teeth.
He cannot make the trunk smooth. He leaves
one night after dark.

3

Roots stiffen under the ground
and the frozen street, coiled around pipes and wires.
The stump is a platform of blond wood
in the gray winter. It is nearly level
with the snow that covers the little garden around it.
It is a door into the underground of old summers,
but if I bend down to it, I am lost
in crags and buttes of a harsh landscape
that goes on forever. When snow melts
the wood darkens into the ground;
rain and thawed snow move deeply into the stump,
backwards along the disused tunnels.

4

The edges of the trunk turn black.
In the middle there is a pale overlay,
like a wash of chalk on darkness.
The desert of the winter
has moved inside.
I do not step on it now; I am used to it,
like a rock, or a bush that does not grow.

There is a sailing ship
beached in the cove of a small island
where the warm water is turquoise.
The hulk leans over, full of rain and sand,
and shore flowers grow from it.
Then it is under full sail in the Atlantic,
on a blue day, heading for the island.

She has planted sweet alyssum
in the holes where the wood was rotten.

It grows thick, it bulges
like flowers contending from a tight vase.
Now the stump sinks downward into its roots
with a cargo of rain
and white blossoms that last into October.

IN THE KITCHEN OF THE OLD HOUSE

In the kitchen of the old house, late,
I was making some coffee
   and I daydreamed sleepily of old friends.
Then the dream turned. I waited.
   I walked alone all day in the town
where I was born. It was cold,
   a Saturday in January
when nothing happens. The streets
   changed as the sky grew dark around me.
The lamps in the small houses
   had tassels on them, and the black cars
at the curb were old and square.
   A ragman passed with his horse, their breaths
blooming like white peonies,
   when I turned into a darker street
and I recognized the house
   from snapshots. I felt as separate
as if the city and the house
   were closed inside a globe which I shook
to make it snow. No sooner
   did I think of snow, but snow started
to fill the heavy darkness
   around me. It reflected the glare
of the streetlight as it fell
   melting on the warmth of the sidewalk

and frozen on frozen grass.
    Then I heard out of the dark the sound
of steps on the bare cement
    in a familiar rhythm. Under
the streetlight, bent to the snow,
    hatless, younger than I, so young that
I was not born, my father
    walked home to his bride and his supper.
A shout gathered inside me
    like a cold wind, to break the rhythm,
to keep him from entering
    that heavy door — but I stood under
a tree, closed in by the snow,
    and did not shout, to tell what happened
in twenty years, in winter,
    when his early death grew inside him
like snow piling on the grass.
    He opened the door and met the young
woman who waited for him.

THE DAYS

Ten years ago this minute, he possibly sat
in the sunlight, in Connecticut, in an old chair;
a car may have stopped in the street outside;
he may have turned his head; his ear may have itched.
Since it was September, he probably saw
single leaves dropping from the maple tree.
If he was reading, he turned back to his book,
and perhaps the smell of roses in a pot
came together with the smell of cheese sandwiches
and the smell of a cigarette
smoked by his brother who was not dead then.

The moments of that day dwindled
to the small notations of clocks,
and the day busily became another day,
and another, and today, when his hand moves
from his ear which still itches
to rest on his leg, it is marked with the passage
of ten years. Suddenly he has the idea
that thousands and thousands of his days
lie stacked into the ground
like leaves, or like that pressure of green
which turns into coal in a million years.

Though leaves rot, or leaves burn in the gutter;
though the complications of this morning's breakfast
dissolve in faint shudders of light
at a great distance, he continues to daydream
that the past is a country under the ground
where the days practice their old habits
over and over, as faint and persistent
as cigarette smoke in an airless room.
He wishes he could travel there like a tourist
and photograph the unseizable days
in the sunlight, in Connecticut, in an old chair.

1966–1969

———————

THE MAN IN THE DEAD MACHINE

High on a slope in New Guinea
the Grumman Hellcat
lodges among bright vines
as thick as arms. In nineteen-forty-three,
the clenched hand of a pilot
glided it here
where no one has ever been.

In the cockpit the helmeted
skeleton sits
upright, held
by dry sinews at neck
and shoulder, and by webbing
that straps the pelvic cross
to the cracked
leather of the seat, and the breastbone
to the canvas cover
of the parachute.

Or say that the shrapnel
missed me, I flew
back to the carrier, and every morning
take the train, my pale
hands on a black case, and sit
upright, held
by the firm webbing.

THE CORNER

It does not know
its name. It sits

in a damp corner,
spit hanging
from its chin, odor of urine
puddled around.
Huge, hairless, grunting,
it plays with itself,
sleeps, stares for hours,
and leaps
to smash itself on the wall.
Limping, bloody, falling back
into the corner, it
will not die.

SWAN

1

December, nightfall at three-thirty.
I climb Mill Hill
past hawthorn and wild cherry,
mist in the hedgerows.
Smoke blows
from the orange edges of fire
working the wheat
stubble. "Putting
the goodness back,
into the soil."

2

Driving; the fog
matted around the headlights;
suddenly, a thudding
white shape in the whiteness,
running huge and frightened, lost
from its slow stream . . .

3

The windmill drew up to power
the dark underneath it
through tunnels like the roots of a beech
up from the center of the earth.
Fire breaks out in the fields
because the wheel of the mill
does not turn.

Fog stacked in the hedges.

The windmill
flies, clattering its huge wings, to the swamp.
I make out cliffs of the church,
houses drifting like glaciers.

4

I envy the man hedging and ditching,
trimming the hawthorn, burning branches
while wasps circle in the smoke of their nest,
clearing a mile of lane, patches of soot
like closed holes to a cave of fire,
the man in his cottage
who smokes his pipe in the winter, in summer
digging his garden in ten o'clock light,
the man grafted entirely to rain and air,
stained dark
by years of hedging and ditching.

5

The close-packed surface of the roots
of a root-bound plant
when I break the pot away,
the edges white
and sleek as a swan . . .

THE ALLIGATOR BRIDE

The clock of my days winds down.
The cat eats sparrows outside my window.
Once, she brought me a small rabbit
which we devoured together, under
the Empire table
while the men shrieked
repossessing the gold umbrella.

Now the beard on my clock turns white.
My cat stares into dark corners
missing her gold umbrella.
She is in love
with the Alligator Bride.

Ah, the tiny fine white
teeth! The Bride, propped on her tail
in white lace
stares from the holes
of her eyes. Her stuck-open mouth
laughs at minister and people.

On bare new wood
fourteen tomatoes,
a dozen ears of corn,
six bottles of white wine,
a melon,
a cat,
broccoli,
and the Alligator Bride.

The color of bubble gum,
the consistency of petroleum jelly,
wickedness oozes
from the palm of my left hand.

My cat licks it.
I watch the Alligator Bride.

Big houses like shabby boulders
hold themselves tight
in gelatin.
I am unable to daydream.
The sky is a gun aimed at me.
I pull the trigger.
The skull of my promises
leans in a black closet, gapes
with its good mouth
for a teat to suck.

A bird flies back and forth
in my house that is covered by gelatin
and the cat leaps at it
missing. Under the Empire table
the Alligator Bride
lies in her bridal shroud.
My left hand
leaks on the Chinese carpet.

THE GRAVE THE WELL

Taking off from Kennedy
in December, from the
airplane, I look at streetlights
below: hovering, unfixed
sockets of light.

Then darkness: Pennsylvania,
Ohio. Yellow headlights

steer slowly along macadam
outstate roads,
far from pianos and theaters.

Women are leaning back in taxis.
Men stoop into taxis
after them, and enter the
grave, the well, the mine
of fur and scent.

SEW

She kneels on the floor, snip snip
in the church of scraps,
tissue like moth's wings,
pins in the cushion of her mouth,
basting and hemming
until it stands up like a person
made out of whole cloth.

Still, I lie folded
on the bolt in the dark warehouse,
dreaming my shapes.

OLD HOUSES

Old houses were scaffolding once
and workmen whistling.

The wrecker's crowbar
splits clapboard and frame;
his chisel piles bricks.
The hole he makes
rain fills. A new apartment
grows from the rain.

The wrecker whistles as loud
as the old whistling that bends
out with the nails.

PICTURES OF PHILIPPA

1
"Here she comes
the Queen of Moons!
and Stars."

With orange hair, blue eyes, and yellow breasts
she floats
smiling
on the triangular balloon
of her dress.

A Star
juts from a pedestal on
top of her head.

2
A pink blob with one red
eye, an orange
pig's nose, blue hair and beard

99

over a yellow mouth: "This
is Daddy when he
was born."

3
The flower sings tenor
under
his black mustache
and sounds come out
yellow; his great head
rises
from a thin stem.

The moon Queen!
stares with her lucid eyes
loving him.

"Goodbye.
Take care of not getting your hair wet."

THE COAL FIRE

A coal fire burned in a basket grate.
We lay in front of it
while ash collected on the firebrick
like snow. The fire was tight and small
and endured
when we added a chunk every hour.
The new piece blazed at first
from the bulky shadow of fire,
turning us bright and dark.

Old coals red at the center
warmed us all night.
If we watched all night
we could not tell the new coal
when it flaked into ash.

THE BLUE WING

She is all around me
like a rainy day,
and though I walk bareheaded
I am not wet. I walk
on a bare path
singing light songs
about women.

A blue wing tilts at the edge of the sea.

The wreck of the small
airplane sleeps
drifted to the high-tide line,
tangled in seaweed, green
glass from the sea.

The tiny skeleton inside
remembers the falter of engines, the
cry without
answer, the long dying
into
and out of the sea.

THE REPEATED SHAPES

I have visited Men's Rooms
in several bars
with the rows
of urinals like old men
and the six-sided odor

of disinfectant.
I have felt the sadness
of the small white tiles,
the repeated shapes
and the unavoidable whiteness.

They are my uncles,
these old men
who are only plumbing,
who throb with tears all night
and doze in the morning.

WOOLWORTH'S

My whole life has led me here.

Daisies made out of resin,
hairnets and submarines,
sandwiches, diaries, green
garden chairs,
and a thousand boxes of cough drops.

Three hundred years ago I was hedging
and ditching in Devon.

I lacked freedom of worship,
and freedom to trade molasses
for rum, for slaves, for molasses.

"I will sail to Massachusetts
to build the Kingdom
of Heaven on Earth!"

The side of a hill
swung open.
It was Woolworth's!

I followed this vision to Boston.

APPLES

They have gone
into the green hill, by doors without hinges,
or lifting city
manhole covers to tunnels
lined with grass,
their skin soft as grapes, their faces like apples.

The peacock
feather, its round eye, sees dancers underground.
The curved spot on this
apple is a fat camel, is a
fly's shadow,
is the cry of a marigold. Looking hard,

I enter:
I am caught in the web of a gray apple,
I struggle inside

an immense apple of blowing sand,
              I blossom
quietly from a window box of apples.

              For one man
there are seven beautiful women with buns
              and happy faces
         in yellow dresses with green sashes
              to bring him
whiskey. The rungs of a ladder tell stories

              to his friend.
Their voices like apples brighten in the wind.
              Now they are dancing
         with fiddles and women and trumpets
              in the round
hill of the peacock, in the resounding hill.

THE TABLE

Walking back to the farm from the depot,
Riley slapped flies with his tail.
Twilight. Crickets scraped
in the green standing hay by the road.
The voice of my grandfather
spoke through a motion of gnats.
I held his hand. I entered
the sway of a horse.
                    At the brown table
I propped books on each other.
All morning in the room my skin
took into itself small discs
of coolness.

Then I walked in the cut hayfield
by the barn, and lay alone
in the little valley of noon heat,
in the village of little sounds.
Grasshoppers
tickled my neck and I let them.
I turned into the other world
that lives in the air. Clouds passed
like motes.
                    My grandfather
clanked up the road on his mowing machine,
behind Riley dark with sweat.
I ran to the barn
and carried a bucket of water
to the loose jaws working
in the dark stall. For lunch
I sliced an onion.
Then we raked hay into mounds
and my grandfather pitched it up
where I tucked it in place on the hayrack.
My skin dried in the sun. Wind
caught me in clover.
The slow ride
back to the barn, I dangled
legs over split-pole rails
while my grandfather talked forever
in a voice that wrapped me around
with love that asked for nothing.
In my room I drank well-water
that whitened the sides of a tumbler
and coolness gathered like dark
inside my stomach.
                    This morning
I walk to the shaded bedroom and lean
on the drop-leaf table.
                    The table hums
a song to itself without sense

and I hear the voice of the heaving
ribs of Riley
and grasshoppers
haying the fields of the air.

MOUNT KEARSARGE

Great blue mountain! Ghost.
I look at you
from the porch of the farmhouse
where I watched you all summer
as a boy. Steep sides, narrow flat
patch on top —
you are clear to me
like the memory of one day.
Blue! Blue!
The top of the mountain floats
in haze.
I will not rock on this porch
when I am old. I turn my back on you,
Kearsarge, I close
my eyes, and you rise inside me,
blue ghost.

1970–1974

GOLD

Pale gold of the walls, gold
of the centers of daisies, yellow roses
pressing from a clear bowl. All day
we lay on the bed, my hand
stroking the deep
gold of your thighs and your back.
We slept and woke
entering the golden room together,
lay down in it breathing
quickly, then
slowly again,
caressing and dozing, your hand sleepily
touching my hair now.

We made in those days
tiny identical rooms inside our bodies
which the men who uncover our graves
will find in a thousand years,
shining and whole.

WATERS

A rock drops in a bucket;
quick fierce
waves exhaust themselves
against the tin circle.

A rock in a pool;
a fast

splash, and ripples move out
interrupted by weeds.

The lake enormous and calm;
a stone falls;
for an hour the surface
moves, holding to itself the frail

shudders of its skin. Stones
on the dark bottom
make the lake calm,
the life worth living.

THE YOUNG WATCH US

The young girls look up
as we walk past the line at the movie,
and go back to examining their fingernails.

Their boyfriends are combing their hair,
and chew gum
as if they meant to insult us.

Today we made love all day.
I look at you. You are smiling at the sidewalk,
dear wrinkled face.

THE DUMP

The trolley has stopped long since.
There is no motorman.

The passenger thinks
he is at the end of the line.
No, he is past the end. Around him
is the graveyard of trolleys,
thousands of oblongs tilted
at angles to each other,
yellow paint chipped.
Stepping outside, he sees smoke rising
from holes in roofs.
Old men live here, in narrow houses full of rugs,
in this last place.

NOSE

it is an accurate nose
like an adding machine
powered by perfect electricity

yet it has no cord
it does not run on batteries

it is an observatory
for observing moons and planets
I watch it revolve

it is a birchbark canoe

it is a snail
that hesitates on a hedge

it is the fist of a new child

it is the egg
of a demonstrable bird
do not sit on this nose

NO COLOR MAN

I lived no-color. In a gray room I talked
clipped whispers
with a woman who faded while I looked at her.
Our voices were oyster-white, my monsters
as pale as puffballs of dust. Leaves of my trees
turned dingy. I mowed pale grass.
Friends parked station wagons like huge dead mice
by my house that was nearly invisible.
Dollar bills lost color
when I kept them in my wallet.
I dreamed of mountains gray like oceans
with no house lights on them,
only coffins that walked and talked
and buried each other continually in gray sand.

STONES

Now it is gone, all of it.
No, it is there,
a rock island twelve miles offshore
in the Atlantic. Straight cliffs,

salt grass on top,
rabbits, snipe.

At lowest tide,
a scrap of sand; maybe once a year
the sea is so calm
that an island man beaches his coracle,
wedges the anchor in stone,
and rock-climbs to the top.

He traps small game,
listening to the wind, fearful
of skull island.
Monks in the Middle Ages
lived in a stone house here
whole lives.

THE HIGH PASTURE

I am the hounds,
I am the fox.

I wake reassembling
torn muscle and fur

to run again
over raw fields

to a corner of stone.
I twitch

awake with the crazy
intolerable scent

of me in my nostrils.
Yet I am also the leaf

that breathes
slowly in sun

by the wooden bridge
at the end of the pond

in the high pasture.

STORIES

I look at the rock and the house;
I look at the boat on the river;
I sit on the colored stone
and listen to stories:

the mountain shudders
at the breath of a lizard
and the stream disappears
in a tunnel of jewels;

the walk of a woman
into darkness stops
when a snake hisses
with the voice of a cavern;

when the rock turns to air
the sun touches
her body, and diamonds
and the talking lake:

cool air at noon,
light on deep water,
fire at night
in the squares of the winter.

TO A WATERFOWL

Women with hats like the rear ends of pink ducks
applauded you, my poems.
These are the women whose husbands I meet on airplanes,
who close their briefcases and ask, "What are *you* in?"
I look in their eyes, I tell them I am in poetry,

and their eyes fill with anxiety, and with little tears.
"Oh, yeah?" they say, developing an interest in clouds.
"My wife, she likes that sort of thing? Hah-hah?
I guess maybe I'd better watch my grammar, huh?"
I leave them in airports, watching their grammar,

and take a limousine to the Women's Goodness Club
where I drink Harvey's Bristol Cream with their wives,
and eat chicken salad with capers, with little tomato wedges,
and I read them "The Erotic Crocodile," and "Eating You."
Ah, when I have concluded the disbursement of sonorities,

crooning, "High on thy thigh I cry, Hi!" — and so forth —
they spank their wide hands, they smile like Jell-O,
and they say, "Hah-hah? My goodness, Mr. Hall,
but you certainly do have an imagination, huh?"
"Thank you, indeed," I say; "it brings in the bacon."

But now, my poems, now I have returned to the motel,
returned to *l'éternel retour* of the Holiday Inn,

naked, lying on the bed, watching *Godzilla Sucks Mt. Fuji,*
addressing my poems, feeling superior, and drinking bourbon
from a flask disguised to look like a transistor radio.

And what about you? You, laughing? You, in the bluejeans,
laughing at your mother who wears hats, and at your father
who rides airplanes with a briefcase watching his grammar?
Will you ever be old and dumb, like your creepy parents?
Not you, not you, not you, not you, not you, not you.

POEM WITH ONE FACT

"At pet stores in Detroit, you can buy
frozen rats
for seventy-five cents apiece, to feed
your pet boa constrictor"
back home in Grosse Pointe,
or in Grosse Pointe Park,

while the free nation of rats
in Detroit emerges
from alleys behind pet shops, from cellars
and junked cars, and gathers
to flow at twilight
like a river the color of pavement,

and crawls over bedrooms and groceries
and through broken
school windows to eat the crayon
from drawings of rats —
and no one in Detroit understands
how rats are delicious in Dearborn.

If only we could *communicate*, if only
the boa constrictors of Southfield
would slither down I-94,
turn north on the Lodge Expressway,
and head for Eighth Street, to eat
out for a change. Instead, tomorrow,

a man from Birmingham enters
a pet shop in Detroit
to buy a frozen German shepherd
for six dollars and fifty cents
to feed his pet cheetah,
guarding the compound at home.

Oh, they arrive all day, in their
locked cars, buying
schoolyards, bridges, buses,
churches, and Ethnic Festivals;
they buy a frozen Texaco station
for eighty-four dollars and fifty cents

to feed to an imported London taxi
in Huntington Woods;
they buy Tiger Stadium,
frozen, to feed to the Little League
in Grosse Ile. They bring everything
home, frozen solid

as pig iron, to the six-car garages
of Harper Woods, Grosse Pointe Woods,
Farmington, Grosse Pointe
Farms, Troy, and Grosse Arbor —
and they ingest
everything, and fall asleep, and lie

coiled in the sun, while the city
thaws in the stomach and slides

to the small intestine, where enzymes
break down molecules of protein
to amino acids, which enter
the cold bloodstream.

THE GREEN SHELF

Driving back from the market,
bags of groceries beside me,
I saw on a lawn
the body of a gray-haired man
twisted beside his power mower.

A woman twisted
her hands above him, mouth wide
with a cry.
She bent close to him, straightened,
bent again, straightened,

and an ambulance
stopped at the curb.
I drove past them slowly
while helpers
kneeled by the man.

Over the stretcher
the lawnmower continued to throb
and absently
the hand of the old woman
caressed the shuddering

handle. Back,
I put the soup cans in order

on the green shelves —
pickles, canned milk, peas,
basil, and tarragon.

FÊTE

Festival lights go on
in villages throughout
   the province, from Toe
Harbor, past the
   Elbow Lakes, to Eyelid Hill
when you touch me, there.

THE PRESIDENTIAD

Abraham Lincoln was giggling uncontrollably. Every few minutes he
was able to stop for breath. Then he began giggling again. He had been
giggling a hundred years. The strain showed terribly in his face. He was
bent over, his knees nearly bumping his chin. He looked like a new mark
of punctuation indicating uncontrollable laughter.

Washington sat with his thumb in his mouth.

Disraeli wore knickers and practiced swinging a golf club. He whistled
frequently, which annoyed Calvin Coolidge, who had affected the dress
of a Prussian general from the 1870 war. Occasionally one of us would see
him pause before a mirror, but none of us took him seriously, nor the
dwarf, who wore shorts and pretended to hunt butterflies.

Jefferson had not spoken since 1845. He appeared to have turned to stone, but regularly every three years a tear moved quickly from the corner of his left eye, and entered his beard, which had grown in 1911, where it evaporated. Several of us speculated that the tear was actually atmospheric, a periodic effect of condensation. But observation confirmed that the tear originated as the secretion of one duct.

The real weeper, however, was Ulysses S. Grant, who wept as continually and uncontrollably as Lincoln giggled. His face was purple, and invariably wet, and he surrounded himself with wet and drying handkerchiefs, which he used in a system of rotation.

ELEANOR'S LETTERS

I who picked up the neat
Old letters never knew
The last names to complete
"Aunt Eleanor" or "Lew."

She talked about the weather,
And canning, and a trip
Which they might take together
"If we don't lose our grip."

But "Lew has got a growth
Which might turn out, they say,
Benign, or shrink, or both."
Then, "Lewis passed away."

He didn't *die*. That word
Seemed harsh and arbitrary

And thus was not preferred
In her vocabulary.

"Everything's for the better,"
She wrote, and what is more,
She signed her dying letter
"As ever, Eleanor."

THE RAISIN

I drank cool water from the fountain
in the undertaker's parlor
near the body of a ninety-two-year-old man.

Harry loved horses and work.
He curried the flanks of his Morgan;
he loaded crates twelve hours — to fill in
when his foreman got drunk —
never kicking a horse,
never kind to a son.

He sobbed on the sofa ten years ago,
when Sally died.
We heard of him dancing
with widows in Florida, cheek
to cheek, and of scented
letters that came to Connecticut
all summer.

When he was old he made up for the weeping
he failed to do earlier —

grandchildren, zinnias,
Morgans, great-grandchildren —
he wept over everything. His only
advice: "Keep your health."
He told old stories, laughing slowly.
He sang old songs.

Forty years ago his son
who was parked making love in the country
noticed Harry parked making love
in a car up ahead.

When he was ninety he wanted to die.
He couldn't ride or grow flowers
or dance
or tend the plots in the graveyard
that he had kept up
faithfully, since Sally died.

This morning I looked into the pale
raisin of Harry's face.

TRANSCONTINENT

Where the cities end, the
dumps grow the oil-can shacks,
from Portland, Maine,

to Seattle. Broken
cars rust in Troy, New York,
and Cleveland Heights.

On the train, the people
eat candy bars, and watch,
or fall asleep.

When they look outside and
see cars and shacks, they know
they're nearly there.

WHITE APPLES

when my father had been dead a week
I woke
with his voice in my ear
                              I sat up in bed
and held my breath
and stared at the pale closed door

white apples and the taste of stone

if he called again
I would put on my coat and galoshes

THE TOWN OF HILL

Back of the dam, under
a flat pad

of water, church
bells ring

in the ears of lilies,
a child's swing

curls in the current
of a yard, horned

pout sleep
in a green

mailbox, and
a boy walks

from a screened
porch beneath

the man-shaped
leaves of an oak

down the street looking
at the town

of Hill that water
covered forty

years ago,
and the screen

door shuts
under dream water.

1975–1978

MAPLE SYRUP

August, goldenrod blowing. We walk
into the graveyard, to find
my grandfather's grave. Ten years ago
I came here last, bringing
marigolds from the round garden
outside the kitchen.
I didn't know you then.
                        We walk
among carved names that go with photographs
on top of the piano at the farm:
Keneston, Wells, Fowler, Batchelder, Buck.
We pause at the new grave
of Grace Fenton, my grandfather's
sister. Last summer
we called on her at the nursing home,
eighty-seven, and nodding
in a blue housedress. We cannot find
my grandfather's grave.
                        Back at the house
where no one lives, we potter
and explore the back chamber
where everything comes to rest: spinning wheels,
pretty boxes, quilts,
bottles, books, albums of postcards.
Then with a flashlight we descend
firm steps to the root cellar — black,
cobwebby, huge,
with dirt floors and fieldstone walls,
and above the walls, holding the hewn
sills of the house, enormous
granite foundation stones.
Past the empty bins
for squash, apples, carrots, and potatoes,

we discover the shelves for canning, a few
pale pints
of tomato left, and — what
is this? — syrup, maple syrup
in a quart jar, syrup
my grandfather made twenty-five
years ago
for the last time.
                    I remember
coming to the farm in March
in sugaring time, as a small boy.
He carried the pails of sap, sixteen-quart
buckets, dangling from each end
of a wooden yoke
that lay across his shoulders, and emptied them
into a vat in the saphouse
where fire burned day and night
for a week.
                    Now the saphouse
tilts, nearly to the ground,
like someone exhausted
to the point of death, and next winter
when snow piles three feet thick
on the roofs of the cold farm,
the saphouse will shudder and slide
with the snow to the ground.
                              Today
we take my grandfather's last
quart of syrup
upstairs, holding it gingerly,
and we wash off twenty-five years
of dirt, and we pull
and pry the lid up, cutting the stiff,
dried rubber gasket, and dip our fingers
in, you and I both, and taste
the sweetness, you for the first time,

the sweetness preserved, of a dead man
in the kitchen he left
when his body slid
like anyone's into the ground.

THE TOY BONE

Looking through boxes
in the attic of my mother's house in Hamden,
I find a model airplane, snapshots
of a dog wearing baby clothes,
a catcher's mitt — the oiled
pocket eaten
by mice — and I discover
the toy bone.

                ✦   ✦   ✦

I sat alone each day
after school, in the living room
of my parents' house in Hamden, ten
years old, eating
slices of plain white bread.
I listened to the record, Connie
Boswell singing
again and again, her voice
turning like a heel, "The Kerry Dancers,"
and I knew she was crippled, and sang
from a wheelchair. I played
with Zippy, my red and white
Shetland collie, throwing
his toy bone

into the air and catching it, or letting it fall,
while he watched me
with intent, curious eyes.

I was happy
in the room dark with the shades drawn.

ILLUSTRATION

In a bookshelf at the dark living room's end
stood the ten volumes of *Journeys Through Bookland*
which my parents bought when I was born.
Sometimes when I was alone in the house

— my mother dressed up and pretty, smelling
of Evening in Paris, playing bridge with other ladies
in silk dresses, their words chosen with care,
speaking of "homes," speaking of "perspiration";

— my father adding columns of figures, his #2
pencil faint on blue-lined, white paper pads,
smoking Chesterfields, coughing at his yellow desk
in the job he hated at Brock-Hall;

— and I in the shaded room, back from broken
chalk on blackboards, from duplicate tables
of multiplication, back from geography's three
implacable colors, from the murderous schoolyard;

I opened a book to the picture beside Longfellow's
poem: stark skull recessed in metal cowl,
sockets glaring like eyes, landscape behind it
empty, inhabited only by "The Skeleton in Armor."

ADULTERY AT FORTY

At the shower's head, high over the porcelain moonscape,
a water drop gathers itself darkly, hangs, shakes, trembles,
and hesitates, uncertain in which direction to hurl itself.

O CHEESE

In the pantry the dear dense cheeses, Cheddars and harsh
Lancashires; Gorgonzola with its magnanimous manner;
the clipped speech of Roquefort; and a head of Stilton
that speaks in a sensuous riddling tongue like Druids.

O cheeses of gravity, cheeses of wistfulness, cheeses
that weep continually because they know they will die.
O cheeses of victory, cheeses wise in defeat, cheeses
fat as a cushion, lolling in bed until noon.

Liederkranz ebullient, jumping like a small dog, noisy;
Pont l'Evêque intellectual, and quite well informed; Emmentaler
decent and loyal, a little deaf in the right ear;
and Brie the revealing experience, instantaneous and profound.

O cheeses that dance in the moonlight, cheeses
that mingle with sausages, cheeses of Stonehenge.
O cheeses that are shy, that linger in the doorway,
eyes looking down, cheeses spectacular as fireworks.

Reblochon openly sexual; Caerphilly like pine trees, small
at the timberline; Port du Salut in love; Caprice des Dieux
eloquent, tactful, like a thousand-year-old hostess;
and Dolcelatte, always generous to a fault.

O village of cheeses, I make you this poem of cheeses,
O family of cheeses, living together in pantries,
O cheeses that keep to your own nature, like a lucky couple,
this solitude, this energy, these bodies slowly dying.

KICKING THE LEAVES

1

Kicking the leaves, October, as we walk home together
from the game, in Ann Arbor,
on a day the color of soot, rain in the air;
I kick at the leaves of maples,
reds of seventy different shades, yellow
like old paper; and poplar leaves, fragile and pale;
and elm leaves, flags of a doomed race.
I kick at the leaves, making a sound I remember
as the leaves swirl upward from my boot,
and flutter; and I remember
Octobers walking to school in Connecticut,
wearing corduroy knickers that swished
with a sound like leaves; and a Sunday buying
a cup of cider at a roadside stand
on a dirt road in New Hampshire; and kicking the leaves,
autumn 1955 in Massachusetts, knowing
my father would die when the leaves were gone.

2

Each fall in New Hampshire, on the farm
where my mother grew up, a girl in the country,
my grandfather and grandmother
finished the autumn work, taking the last vegetables in
from the cold fields, canning, storing roots and apples
in the cellar under the kitchen. Then my grandfather

raked leaves against the house
as the final chore of autumn.
One November I drove up from college to see them.
We pulled big rakes, as we did when we hayed in summer,
pulling the leaves against the granite foundations
around the house, on every side of the house,
and then, to keep them in place, we cut spruce boughs
and laid them across the leaves,
green on red, until the house
was tucked up, ready for snow
that would freeze the leaves in tight, like a stiff skirt.
Then we puffed through the shed door,
taking off boots and overcoats, slapping our hands,
and sat in the kitchen, rocking, and drank
black coffee my grandmother made,
three of us sitting together, silent, in gray November.

3

One Saturday when I was little, before the war,
my father came home at noon from his half day at the office
and wore his Bates sweater, black on red,
with the crossed hockey sticks on it, and raked beside me
in the back yard, and tumbled in the leaves with me,
laughing, and carried me, laughing, my hair full of leaves,
to the kitchen window
where my mother could see us, and smile, and motion
to set me down, afraid I would fall and be hurt.

4

Kicking the leaves today, as we walk home together
from the game, among crowds of people
with their bright pennants, as many and bright as leaves,
my daughter's hair is the red-yellow color
of birch leaves, and she is tall like a birch,
growing up, fifteen, growing older; and my son
flamboyant as maple, twenty,
visits from college, and walks ahead of us, his step

springing, impatient to travel
the woods of the earth. Now I watch them
from a pile of leaves beside this clapboard house
in Ann Arbor, across from the school
where they learned to read,
as their shapes grow small with distance, waving,
and I know that I
diminish, not them, as I go first
into the leaves, taking
the way they will follow, Octobers and years from now.

5

This year the poems came back, when the leaves fell.
Kicking the leaves, I heard the leaves tell stories,
remembering, and therefore looking ahead, and building
the house of dying. I looked up into the maples
and found them, the vowels of bright desire.
I thought they had gone forever
while the bird sang *I love you, I love you*
and shook its black head
from side to side, and its red eye with no lid,
through years of winter, cold
as the taste of chickenwire, the music of cinderblock.

6

Kicking the leaves, I uncover the lids of graves.
My grandfather died at seventy-seven, in March
when the sap was running; and I remember my father
twenty years ago,
coughing himself to death at fifty-two in the house
in the suburbs. Oh, how we flung
leaves in the air! How they tumbled and fluttered around us,
like slowly cascading water, when we walked together
in Hamden, before the war, when Johnson's Pond
had not surrendered to houses, the two of us
hand in hand, and in the wet air the smell of leaves

burning;
and in six years I will be fifty-two.

7
Now I fall, now I leap and fall
to feel the leaves crush under my body, to feel my body
buoyant in the ocean of leaves, the night of them,
night heaving with death and leaves, rocking like the ocean.
Oh, this delicious falling into the arms of leaves,
into the soft laps of leaves!
Face down, I swim into the leaves, feathery,
breathing the acrid odor of maple, swooping
in long glides to the bottom of October —
where the farm lies curled against winter, and soup steams
its breath of onion and carrot
onto damp curtains and windows; and past the windows
I see the tall bare maple trunks and branches, the oak
with its few brown weathery remnant leaves,
and the spruce trees, holding their green.
Now I leap and fall, exultant, recovering
from death, on account of death, in accord with the dead,
the smell and taste of leaves again,
and the pleasure, the only long pleasure, of taking a place
in the story of leaves.

EATING THE PIG

Twelve people, most of us strangers, stand in a room
in Ann Arbor, drinking Cribari from jars.
Then two young men, who cooked him,
carry him to the table
on a large square of plywood: his body
striped, like a tiger cat's, from the basting,

his legs long, much longer than a cat's,
and the striped hide as shiny as vinyl.

Now I see his head, as he takes his place
at the center of the table,
his wide pig's head; and he looks like the *javelina*
that ran in front of the car, in the desert outside Tucson,
and I am drawn to him, my brother the pig,
with his large ears cocked forward,
with his tight snout, with his small ferocious teeth
in a jaw propped open
by an apple. How bizarre, this raw apple clenched
in a cooked face! Then I see his eyes,
his eyes cramped shut, his no-eyes, his eyes like X's
in a comic strip, when the character gets knocked out.

This afternoon they read directions
from a book: *The eyeballs must be removed*
or they will burst during roasting. So they hacked them out.
"I nearly fainted," says someone.
"I never fainted before, in my whole life."
Then they gutted the pig and stuffed him,
and roasted him five hours, basting the long body.

    ✎   ✎   ✎

Now we examine him, exclaiming, and we marvel at him —
but no one picks up a knife.

Then a young woman cuts off his head.
It comes off so easily, like a detachable part.
With sudden enthusiasm we dismantle the pig,
we wrench his trotters off, we twist them
at shoulder and hip, and they come off so easily.
Then we cut open his belly and pull the skin back.

For myself, I scoop a portion of left thigh,
moist, tender, falling apart, fat, sweet.

We forage like an army starving in winter
that crosses a pass in the hills and discovers
a valley of full barns —
cattle fat and lowing in their stalls,
bins of potatoes in root cellars under white farmhouses,
barrels of cider, onions, hens squawking over eggs —
and the people nowhere, with bread still warm in the oven.

Maybe, south of the valley, refugees pull their carts
listening for Stukas or elephants, carrying
bedding, pans, and silk dresses,
old men and women, children, deserters, young wives.

No, we are here, eating the pig together.

                ✦   ✦   ✦

In ten minutes, the destruction is total.

His tiny ribs, delicate as birds' feet, lie crisscrossed.
Or they are like crosshatching in a drawing,
lines doubling and redoubling on each other.

Bits of fat and muscle
mix with stuffing alien to the body,
walnuts and plums. His skin, like a parchment bag
soaked in oil, is pulled back and flattened,
with ridges and humps remaining, like a contour map,
like the map of a defeated country.

The army consumes every blade of grass in the valley,
every tree, every stream, every village,
every crossroad, every shack, every book, every graveyard.

His intact head
swivels around, to view the landscape of body
as if in dismay.

"For sixteen weeks I lived. For sixteen weeks
I took into myself nothing but the milk of my mother
who rolled on her side for me,
for my brothers and sisters. Only five hours roasting,
and this body so quickly dwindles away to nothing."

      ✦   ✦   ✦

By itself, isolated on this plywood,
among this puzzle of foregone possibilities,
his intact head seems to want affection.
Without knowing that I will do it,
I reach out and scratch his jaw,
and I stroke him behind his ears,
as if he might suddenly purr from his cooked head.

"When I stroke your pig's ears,
and scratch the striped leather of your jowls,
the furrow between the sockets of your eyes,
I take into myself, and digest,
wheat that grew between
the Tigris and the Euphrates rivers.

"And I take into myself the flint carving tool,
and the savannah, and hairs in the tail
of Eohippus, and fingers of bamboo,
and Hannibal's elephant, and Hannibal,
and everything that lived before us, everything born,
exalted, and dead, and historians
who carved in the Old Kingdom
when the wall had not heard about China."

I speak these words
into the ear of the Stone Age pig, the Abraham
pig, the ocean pig, the Achilles pig,
and into the ears
of the fire pig that will eat our bodies up.

"Fire, brother and father,
twelve of us, in our different skins, older and younger,
opened your skin together
and tore your body apart, and took it
into our bodies."

WOLF KNIFE

> from *The Journals of*
> C. F. Hoyt, USN, 1826–1889

"In mid-August, in the second year
of my First Polar Expedition, the snows and ice of winter
almost upon us, Kantiuk and I
attempted to dash by sledge
along Crispin Bay, searching again for relics
of the Franklin Expedition. Now a storm blew,
and we turned back, and we struggled slowly
in snow, lest we depart land and venture onto ice
from which a sudden fog and thaw
would abandon us to the Providence
of the sea.

                              "Near nightfall
I thought I heard snarling behind us.
Kantiuk told me
that two wolves, lean as the bones
of a wrecked ship,
had followed us the last hour, and snapped their teeth
as if already feasting.
I carried but the one charge
in my rifle, since, approaching the second winter,
we rationed stores.

"As it turned dark,
we could push no farther, and made
camp in a corner
of ice-hummocks,
and the wolves stopped also, growling
just past the limits of vision,
coming closer, until I could hear
the click of their feet on ice. Kantiuk laughed
and remarked that the wolves appeared to be most hungry.
I raised my rifle, prepared to shoot the first
that ventured close, hoping
to frighten the other.

"Kantiuk struck my rifle
down, and said again
that the wolves were hungry, and laughed.
I feared that my old companion
was mad, here in the storm, among ice-hummocks,
stalked by wolves. Now Kantiuk searched
in his pack, and extricated
two knives — *turnoks,* the Innuits called them —
which by great labor were sharpened, on both sides,
to a sharpness like the edge of a barber's razor,
and approached our dogs
and plunged both knives
into the body of our youngest dog
who had limped all day.

"I remember
that I considered turning my rifle on Kantiuk
as he approached, then passed me,
carrying knives red with the gore of our dog —
who had yowled, moaned, and now lay
expiring, surrounded
by curious cousins and uncles,
possibly hungry — and thrust the knives
handle-down in the snow.

"Immediately
he left the knives, the vague, gray
shapes of the wolves
turned solid, out of the darkness and the snow,
and set ravenously
to licking blood from the honed steel.
The double edge of the knives
so lacerated the tongues of the starved beasts
that their own blood poured
copiously forth
to replenish the dog's blood, and they ate
more furiously than before, while Kantiuk laughed,
and held his sides
laughing.

        "And I laughed also,
perhaps in relief that Providence had delivered us
yet again, or perhaps — under conditions of extremity,
far from Connecticut — finding these creatures
acutely ridiculous, so avid
to swallow their own blood. First one, and then the other
collapsed, dying,
bloodless in the snow black with their own blood,
and Kantiuk retrieved
his *turnoks,* and hacked lean meat
from the thigh of the larger wolf,
which we ate
gratefully, blessing the Creator, for we were hungry."

PHOTOGRAPHS OF CHINA

After the many courses, hot bowls of rice,
plates of pork, cabbage, duck, and peapods,

we return to Chia-Shun's living room,
to the fire and conversation.
                                    Chia-Shun brings over
an old book of photographs, printed in France.
"I want to show you China," he says,
"our China. This river" — he spreads a page flat —
"my university was beside this river."
The river looks wide, in the sepia photograph,
maybe half a mile wide, geese floating on it, and junks.
Beyond the river, there are rolling darkening hills,
like elephant skin, like the brows of Indian elephants.

"During the war, we bathed ourselves in that river.
Oh, it was cold in the winter!"

      ✦   ✦   ✦

Li Chi crosses the room, touching the furniture.
She sits on the sofa between us, and peers
into the pages of photographs, her glasses
nearly bumping the pages she turns.
"Here," she says, "is West Lake, which is my home.
I always lived near the water, until now,
in Ann Arbor." Her laugh makes a noise like paper.

"When I was first at the university, in China,
I lived so close to the water
that I could fish out my window!"
                                    Later,
we will persuade her to sing a poem from T'ang
that she learned from her mother, in her mother's accents.

      ✦   ✦   ✦

We sit on the sofa, turning the pages together.
When we come to the river again, the book lies flat,
and Chia-Shun says,
                        "On Sundays,
I would ask my friend to help me prepare my assignment.

Then I spent all day
walking alone in the mountains."
                              There were orange trees
beside the hot springs, even in frosty winter.

"How the gold shone in the green shadows then!"

            ✓   ✓   ✓

"When I was teaching," Li Chi says, "in another city,
the planes bombed the house where I lived.
Fortunately, I was not home at the time" — she laughs —
"but my clothes, *all* of my clothes,
were up in a tree."
                    Chia-Shun laughs also,
and closes the book, and says,
"When I see these pictures, when I remember these things"
— he looks like a boy, wild and pink with excitement —
"I want to live two hundred years!"

                              And Li Chi:
"When I close my eyes, because my eyes hurt me,
then it is West Lake that I see."

ON REACHING THE AGE OF
TWO HUNDRED

When I awoke on the morning
of my two hundredth birthday,
I expected to be consulted
by supplicants
like the Sibyl at Cumae.
I could tell them something.

143

Instead, it was the usual thing:
dried grapefruit for breakfast,
Mozart all morning, interrupted
by bees' wings,
and making love with a woman
one hundred and eighty-one years old.

At my birthday party
I blew out two hundred candles
one at a time, taking
naps after each twenty-five.
Then I went to bed, at five-thirty,
on the day of my two hundredth birthday,

and slept and dreamed
of a house no bigger than a flea's house
with two hundred rooms in it,
and in each of the rooms a bed,
and in each of the two hundred beds
me sleeping.

FLIES

A fly sleeps on the field of a green curtain. I sit by my grandmother's side, and rub her head as if I could comfort her. Ninety-seven years. Her eyes stay closed, her mouth open, and she gasps in her blue nightgown — pale blue, washed a thousand times. Now her face goes white, and her breath slows until I think it has stopped; then she gasps again, and pink returns to her face.

Between the roof of her mouth and her tongue, strands of spittle waver as she breathes. Now a nurse shakes her head over my grandmother's sore mouth, and goes to get a glass of water, a spoon, and a flyswatter. My grandmother chokes on a spoonful of water and the nurse swats the fly.

✓   ✓   ✓

In the Connecticut suburbs where I grew up, and in Ann Arbor, there were houses with small leaded panes, where Formica shone in the kitchens, and hardwood in closets under paired leather boots. Carpets lay thick underfoot in every bedroom, bright, clean, with no dust or hair in them. Nothing looked used, in these houses. Forty dollars' worth of cut flowers leaned from Waterford vases for the Saturday dinner party.

Even in houses like these, the housefly wandered and paused — and I listened for the buzz of its wings and its tiny feet, as it struggled among cut flowers and bumped into leaded panes.

✓   ✓   ✓

In the afternoon my mother takes over at my grandmother's side in the Peabody Home, while I go back to the farm. I nap in the room my mother and my grandmother were born in.

At night we assemble beside her. Her shallow, rapid breath rasps, and her eyes jerk, and the nurse can find no pulse, as her small strength concentrates wholly on half an inch of lung space, and she coughs faintly — quick coughs like fingertips on a ledge. Her daughters stand by the bed, solemn in the slow evening, in the shallows of after-supper — Caroline, Nan, and Lucy, her eldest daughter, seventy-two, who holds her hand to help her die, as twenty years past she did the same thing for my father.

Then her breath slows again, as it has done all day. Pink vanishes from cheeks we have kissed so often, and her nostrils quiver. She breathes one more quick breath. Her mouth twitches sharply, as if she speaks a word we cannot hear. Her face is fixed, white, her eyes half closed, and the next breath never comes.

✓   ✓   ✓

She lies in a casket covered with gray linen, which my mother and her sisters picked. This is Chadwick's Funeral Parlor in New London, on the ground floor under the I.O.O.F. Her fine hair lies combed on the pillow. Her teeth in, her mouth closed, she looks the way she used to, except that her face is tinted, tanned as if she worked in the fields.

This air is so still it has bars. Because I have been thinking about flies,

145

I realize that there are no flies in this room. I imagine a fly wandering in, through these dark-curtained windows, to land on my grandmother's nose.

At the Andover graveyard, Astroturf covers the dirt next to the shaft dug for her. Mr. Jones says a prayer beside the open hole. He preached at the South Danbury Church when my grandmother still played the organ. He raises his narrow voice, which gives itself over to August and blue air, and tells us that Kate in heaven "will keep on growing . . . and growing . . . and growing" — and he stops abruptly, as if the sky had abandoned him, and chose to speak elsewhere through someone else.

✶   ✶   ✶

After the burial I walk by myself in the barn where I spent summers next to my grandfather. I think of them talking in heaven. Her first word is the word her mouth was making when she died.

In this tie-up a chaff of flies roiled in the leather air, as my grandfather milked his Holsteins morning and night, his bald head pressed sweating into their sides, fat female Harlequins, while their black and white tails swept back and forth, stirring the flies up. His voice spoke pieces he learned for the Lyceum, and I listened crouched on a three-legged stool, as his hands kept time *strp strp* with alternate streams of hot milk, the sound softer as milk foamed to the pail's top.

In the tie-up the spiders feasted like emperors. Each April he broomed the webs out and whitewashed the wood, but spiders and flies came back, generation on generation — like the cattle, mothers and daughters, for a hundred and fifty years, until my grandfather's heart flapped in his chest. One by one the slow Holsteins climbed the ramp into a cattle truck.

✶   ✶   ✶

In the kitchen with its bare hardwood floor, my grandmother stood by the clock's mirror to braid her hair every morning. She looked out the window toward Kearsarge, and said, "Mountain's pretty today," or, "Can't see the mountain too good today."

She fought the flies all summer. She shut the screen door *quickly,* but flies gathered on canisters, on the clockface, on the range when the fire was out, on set-tubs, tables, curtains, chairs. Flies buzzed on cooling lard, when my grandmother made doughnuts. Flies lit on a drip of jam before she could wipe it up. Flies whirled over simmering beans, in the steam of maple syrup.

146

My grandmother fretted, and took good aim with a flyswatter, and hung strips of flypaper behind the range where nobody would tangle her hair in it.

She gave me a penny for every ten I killed. All day with my mesh flyswatter I patrolled kitchen and dining room, living room, even the dead air of the parlor. Though I killed every fly in the house by bedtime, when my grandmother washed the hardwood floor, by morning their sons and cousins assembled in the kitchen, like the woodchucks my grandfather shot in the vegetable garden which doubled and returned; or like the deer that watched for a hundred and fifty years from the brush on Ragged Mountain, and when my grandfather died stalked down the mountainside to graze among peas and corn.

✐ ✐ ✐

We live in their house with our books and pictures, writing poems under Ragged Mountain, gazing each morning at blue Kearsarge.

We live in the house left behind; we sleep in the bed where they whispered together at night. One morning I wake hearing a voice from sleep: "The blow of the axe resides in the acorn."

I get out of bed and drink cold water in the dark morning from the sink's dipper at the window under the sparse oak, and a fly wakes buzzing beside me, cold, and sweeps over set-tubs and range, one of the hundred-thousandth generation.

I planned long ago I would live here, somebody's grandfather.

OX CART MAN

In October of the year,
he counts potatoes dug from the brown field,
counting the seed, counting
the cellar's portion out,
and bags the rest on the cart's floor.

147

He packs wool sheared in April, honey
in combs, linen, leather
tanned from deerhide,
and vinegar in a barrel
hooped by hand at the forge's fire.

He walks by his ox's head, ten days
to Portsmouth Market, and sells potatoes,
and the bag that carried potatoes,
flaxseed, birch brooms, maple sugar, goose
feathers, yarn.

When the cart is empty he sells the cart.
When the cart is sold he sells the ox,
harness and yoke, and walks
home, his pockets heavy
with the year's coin for salt and taxes,

and at home by fire's light in November cold
stitches new harness
for next year's ox in the barn,
and carves the yoke, and saws planks
building the cart again.

STONE WALLS

I

Stone walls emerge from leafy ground
and show their bones. In September a leaf
falls singly down, then a thousand leaves whirl
in frosty air. I am wild
with joy of leaves falling, of stone walls
emerging, of return to the countryside

where I lay as a boy
in the valley of noon heat, in the village
of little sounds; where I floated
out of myself, into the world that lives in the air.

In October the leaves turn
on low hills in middle distance, like heather, like tweed,
like tweed woven from heather and gorse,
purples, greens, reds, grays, oranges, weaving together
this joyful fabric,
and I walk in the afternoon sun, kicking the leaves.

In November the brightness washes from the hills
and I love the land most, leaves down, color drained out
in November rain,
everything gray and brown, against the dark evergreen,
everything rock and silver, lichen and moss on stone,
strong bones of stone walls showing at last
in November cold,
making wavy rectangles on the unperishing hills.

2

Wesley Wells was my grandfather's name.
He had high cheekbones, and laughed as he hoed,
practicing his stories.

The first time I remember him, it was summer at twilight.
He was weak from flu, and couldn't hike for his cows
on Ragged Mountain; he carried the old chair with no back
that he used for milking
to the hillside over the house and called up-mountain:
"Ke-bosh, ke-bosh, ke-bo-o-o-sh, ke-bosh . . ."

ʄ   ʄ   ʄ

While he milked he told about drummers and base-ball;
he recited Lyceum poems about drunk deacons,
or about Lawyer Green, whose skin was the color green,

ridiculed as a schoolboy, who left town and returned triumphant;
and riding home from the hayfields, he handed me the past:
how he walked on a row of fenceposts
in the blizzard of eighty-eight; or sawed oblongs
of ice from Eagle Pond; or in summer
drove the hayrack into shallow water, swelling wooden
wheels tight inside iron rims;
or chatted and teased outside Amos Johnson's with Buffalo Billy
Fiske who dressed like a cowboy.

While I daydreamed my schoolyear life
at Spring Glen Grammar School, or Hamden High,
I longed to return to him, in his awkward coat and cap,
in his sweater with many holes.

　　3
A century ago these hills were bare;
you could see past Eagle Pond to sheep in the far pasture,
walls crossing cleared land, keeping Keneston
lambs from Peasly potatoes.

Today I walk in fields grown over — among
bare birches, oak saplings, enormous
sugarmaples gone into themselves for winter —
beside granite that men stacked
"for twenty-five cents a rod, and forage
for oxen," boulders sledded into place,
smaller stones
fitted by clever hands to lock together, like the arched
ramparts at Mycenae.

I come to the foundations of an abandoned mill;
at the two sides of a trout stream, fieldstone walls emerging
uncut and unmortared
rear like a lion gate,
　　　　　　　　　emptiness over
the still-rushing waters.

4

Allende's murderers follow Orlando Letelier
to Washington; they blow up his car by remote control.
His scream is distant, like the grocer's scream
stabbed in the holdup. These howls —
and Tsvetayeva's in Yelabuga,
who hangs herself in her cottage —
                                        pulse, reverberate, and die
in the scrub pine that grows from granite ledges
visible against snow at the top of Kearsarge,
because jamming plates drove
the Appalachian range through the earth crust
before men and women, before squirrels, before spruce and daisies,
when only amoebas wept
to divide from themselves. Stone dwindled
under millennial rain
like snowbanks in March, and diminished under glaciers,
under the eyes of mice and reindeer, under the eyes of foxes,
under Siberian eyes
tracking bear ten thousand years ago
on Kearsarge;
                and the Shah of Iran's opponents
wake to discover nails
driven through their kneecaps. When Pinochet frowns
in Chile, hearing these howls,
the corners of his mouth twitch with an uncontrollable grin;
Tiberius listening grins.
                                Each morning we watch stone walls
emerge on Kearsarge and on Ragged Mountain;
I love these mountains which do not change.
The screams persist. I continue my life.

5

At Thornley's Store,
the dead mingle with the living; Benjamin Keneston hovers
with Wesley among hardware; Kate looks over spools of thread
with Nanny; and old shadows stand among dowels and raisins,

woolen socks and axes. Now Ansel stops to buy salt
and tells Bob Thornley it got so cold he saw
two hounddogs put jumper cables on a jackrabbit.
Skiers stop for gas; summer people join us, hitchhikers,
roadworkers, machinists, farmers, saw-sharpeners;
our cries and hungers, stories and music, reverberate
on the hills and stone walls, on the Exxon sign and clapboard
of Thornley's Store.

6

At church we eat squares of bread, we commune with mothers
and cousins, with mothering-fathering hills, with dead and living,
and go home in gray November, in Advent waiting,
among generations unborn
who will look at the same hills, as the leaves fall and turn gray,
and watch stone walls ascending Ragged Mountain.

ᔕ　　　ᔕ　　　ᔕ

These walls are the bones of Presidents, men and women
who were never born
and will never lead the Republic into the valley of cattle.

ᔕ　　　ᔕ　　　ᔕ

When gangs fight with dogs for the moose's body,
and poems for Letelier are scattered like the molecules of his body,
and the books are burnt, and this room wet ashes, and language
burnt out, and the dead departed along with the living,
wavering stone lines
will emerge from leaves in November, on mountains without names.

ᔕ　　　ᔕ　　　ᔕ

Pole beans raise their green flags in the summer garden.
I grow old, in the house I wanted to grow old in.
When I am sleepy at night, I daydream only
of waking the next morning — to walk on the earth of the present
past noons of birch and sugarbush, past cellarholes,
many miles to the village of nightfall.

OLD ROSES

White roses, tiny and old, flare among thorns
by the barn door.
     For a hundred years
under the June elm, under the gaze
of seven generations,
      they lived briefly
like this, in the month of roses,
        by the fields
stout with corn, or with clover and timothy
making thick hay,
      grown over, now,
with milkweed, sumac, paintbrush.
          Old

roses survive
winter drifts, the melt in April, August
parch,
   and men and women
who sniffed roses in spring and called them pretty
as we call them now,
      walking beside the barn
on a day that perishes.

TRAFFIC

Trucks and station wagons, VWs, old Chevys, Pintos,
drive stop-and-go down Whitney Avenue this hot
May day, bluing the coarse air, past graveyard and florist,
past this empty brick building covered
with ivy like a Mayan temple,

like a pyramid grown over with jungle vines.

　　　　　　　　　　　I walk around
the building as if I were dreaming it; as if
I had left my planet at twenty
and wandered a lifetime among galaxies and come home
to find my planet aged ten thousand years,
ruined, grown over,
the people gone, ruin taking their places.

　　　　　　　　　　　　　They
have gone into graveyards, who worked at this loading dock
wearing brown uniforms with the pink and blue lettering
of the Brock-Hall Dairy:
Freddie Bauer is dead, who watched over the stockroom;
Agnes McSparren is dead, who wrote figures in books
at a yellow wooden desk; Harry Bailey is dead,
who tested for bacteria
wearing a white coat; Karl Kapp is dead,
who loaded his van at dawn,
conveyorbelt supplying butter, cottage cheese, heavy cream,
B, buttermilk, A with its creamline —
and left white bottles at backdoors in North Haven and Hamden
for thirty years; my father is dead
and my grandfather.

　　　　　　　　I stand by the fence at lot's end
where the long stable stood —
fifty workhorses alive
in the suburbs, chestnuts with thick manes, their hooves
the size of oak stumps, that pulled forty thousand quarts
through mists in the early morning to sleeping doorsteps,
until new trucks jammed the assembly lines
when the war ended.

　　　　　　　　　　I separate ivy
like long hair over a face
to gaze into the room where the bottlewasher
stretched its aluminum length like an Airstream trailer.
When our teacher brought the first grade to the dairy,

men in white caps stacked dirty bottles
at the machine's end, and we heard them clink
forty feet to where they rode out shining
on a belt to another machine
that turned them instantly white, as if someone said a word
that turned them white. I was proud
of my father and grandfather,
of my last name.
               Here is the place
that was lettered with my father's name,
where he parked his Oldsmobile in the fifties.
I came to the plant with him one summer
when I was at college, and we walked across blacktop
where people my age washed trucks;
both of us smiled and looked downwards. That year
the business grossed sixteen million dollars
with four hundred people bottling and delivering milk
and Agnes McSparren was boss
over thirty women.
               At the roof's edge,
imperial Roman cement urns
flourish and decorate exhausted air.
Now suburbs have migrated north
leaving Whitneyville behind, with its dead factory
beside a dead movie. They lived in Whitneyville
mostly — Freddie Bauer, Agnes McSparren, Karl Kapp,
Harry Bailey — who walked their lives
into brick, whose hours turned into milk,
who left their lives inside pitted brick
that disappears beneath ivy
for a thousand years, until the archeologist from a far galaxy
chops with his machete . . .
               No, no, no.
In a week or a year
the wrecker's derrick with fifteen-ton cement ball
on a flatbed trailer

will stop traffic as it squeezes up Whitney Avenue,
and brick will collapse, and dump trucks take clean fill
for construction rising from a meadow
ten miles in the country.
                              I wait
for the traffic to pause, shift, and enter the traffic.

THE BLACK-FACED SHEEP

Ruminant pillows! Gregarious soft boulders!

If one of you found a gap in a stone wall,
the rest of you — rams, ewes, bucks, wethers, lambs;
mothers and daughters, old grandfather-father,
cousins and aunts, small bleating sons —
followed onward, stupid
as sheep, wherever
your leader's sheep-brain wandered to.

My grandfather spent all day searching the valley
and edges of Ragged Mountain,
calling "Ke-*day!*" as if he brought you salt,
"Ke-*day!* Ke-*day!*"

                    *   *   *

When the shirt wore out, and darns in the woolen
shirt needed darning,
a woman in a white collar
cut the shirt into strips and braided it,
as she braided her hair every morning.

In a hundred years
the knees of her great-granddaughter

crawled on a rug made from the wool of sheep
whose bones were mud,
like the bones of the woman, who stares
from an oval in the parlor.

✦   ✦   ✦

I forked the brambly hay down to you
in nineteen-fifty. I delved my hands deep
in the winter grass of your hair.

When the shearer cut to your nakedness in April
and you dropped black eyes in shame,
hiding in barnyard corners, unable to hide,
I brought grain to raise your spirits,
and ten thousand years
wound us through pasture and hayfield together,
threads of us woven
together, three hundred generations
from Africa's hills to New Hampshire's.

✦   ✦   ✦

You were not shrewd like the pig.
You were not strong like the horse.
You were not brave like the rooster.

Yet none of the others looked like a lump of granite
that grew hair,
and none of the others
carried white fleece as soft as dandelion seed
around a black face,
and none of them sang such a flat and sociable song.

✦   ✦   ✦

Now the black-faced sheep have wandered and will not return,
even if I should search the valleys
and call "Ke-*day*," as if I brought them salt.

Now the railroad draws
a line of rust through the valley. Birch, pine, and maple
lean from cellarholes
and cover the dead pastures of Ragged Mountain
except where machines make snow
and cables pull money up hill, to slide back down.

      ✦   ✦   ✦

At South Danbury Church twelve of us sit —
cousins and aunts, sons —
where the great-grandfathers of the forty-acre farms
filled every pew.
I look out the window at summer places,
at Boston lawyers' houses
with swimming pools cunningly added to cowsheds,
and we read an old poem aloud, about Israel's sheep,
old lumps of wool, and we read

that the rich farmer, though he names his farm for himself,
takes nothing into his grave;
that even if people praise us, because we are successful,
we will go under the ground
to meet our ancestors collected there in the darkness;
that we are all of us sheep, and death is our shepherd,
and we die as the animals die.

NAMES OF HORSES

All winter your brute shoulders strained against collars, padding
and steerhide over the ash hames, to haul
sledges of cordwood for drying through spring and summer,
for the Glenwood stove next winter, and for the simmering range.

In April you pulled cartloads of manure to spread on the fields,
dark manure of Holsteins, and knobs of your own clustered with oats.
All summer you mowed the grass in meadow and hayfield, the mowing
   machine
clacketing beside you, while the sun walked high in the morning;

and after noon's heat, you pulled a clawed rake through the same acres,
gathering stacks, and dragged the wagon from stack to stack,
and the built hayrack back, up hill to the chaffy barn,
three loads of hay a day, hanging wide from the hayrack.

Sundays you trotted the two miles to church with the light load
of a leather quartertop buggy, and grazed in the sound of hymns.
Generation on generation, your neck rubbed the window sill
of the stall, smoothing the wood as the sea smooths glass.

When you were old and lame, when your shoulders hurt bending to graze,
one October the man who fed you and kept you, and harnessed you every
   morning,
led you through corn stubble to sandy ground above Eagle Pond,
and dug a hole beside you where you stood shuddering in your skin,

and lay the shotgun's muzzle in the boneless hollow behind your ear,
and fired the slug into your brain, and felled you into your grave,
shoveling sand to cover you, setting goldenrod upright above you,
where by next summer a dent in the ground made your monument.

For a hundred and fifty years, in the pasture of dead horses,
roots of pine trees pushed through the pale curves of your ribs,
yellow blossoms flourished above you in autumn, and in winter
frost heaved your bones in the ground — old toilers, soil makers:

O Roger, Mackerel, Riley, Ned, Nellie, Chester, Lady Ghost.

1979–1986

———————

GREAT DAY IN THE COWS' HOUSE

In the dark tie-up seven huge Holsteins
lower their heads to feed, chained loosely to old saplings
with whitewashed bark still on them.
They are long dead; they survive, in the great day
that cancels the successiveness of creatures.
Now she stretches her wrinkly neck, her turnip eye
rolls in her skull, she sucks up breath,
and stretching her long mouth mid-chew she expels:
mm-mmm-mmmmm-mmmmmmmm-ugghwanchhh.
— Sweet bellowers enormous and interchangeable,
your dolorous ululations
swell out barnsides, fill spaces inside haymows,
resound down valleys. Moos of revenant cattle
shake ancient timbers and timbers still damp with sap.

      ✶   ✶   ✶

Now it is warm, late June. The old man strokes
white braids of milk, *strp strp,* from ruminant beasts
with hipbones like tentpoles, the rough
black-and-white hanging crudely upon them.
Now he tilts back his head to recite a poem
about an old bachelor who loves a chicken named Susan.
His voice grows loud with laughter and emphasis
in the silent tie-up where old noises gather.

      ✶   ✶   ✶

Now a tail lifts to waterfall huge and yellow
or an enormous flop presses out. Done milking, he lifts
with his hoe a leather-hinged board
to scrape manure onto the pile underneath, in April
carted for garden and fieldcorn.
                    The cows in their house
decree the seasons; spring seeds corn,

summer hays, autumn fences, and winter saws ice
from Eagle Pond, sledging it up hill to pack it away
in sawdust; through August's parch and Indian summer
great chunks of the pond float in the milkshed tank.

✦   ✦   ✦

Pull down the spiderwebs! Whitewash the tie-up!
In the great day there is also the odor of poverty
and anxiety over the Agricultural Inspector's visit.

✦   ✦   ✦

They are long dead; they survive, in the great day
of August, to convene afternoon and morning
for milking. Now they graze Ragged Mountain: —
steep sugarbush, little mountain valleys and brooks,
high clovery meadows, slate-colored lowbush blueberries.
When grass is sweetest they are slow to leave it;
late afternoons he spends hours searching.
He knows their secret places; he listens for one peal
of a cowbell carried on a breeze; he calls:
"Ke-bosh, ke-bo-o-sh, ke-bosh, ke-bosh . . ."
He climbs dry creekbeds and old logging roads
or struggles up needle-banks pulling on fir branches.
He hacks with his jackknife a chunk of sprucegum
oozing from bark and softens it in his cheek-pouch
for chewing.
            Then he pushes through hemlock's gate
to join the society of Holsteins; they look up from grass
as if mildly surprised, and file immediately downwards.

✦   ✦   ✦

Late in October after the grass freezes
the cattle remain in their stalls, twice a day loosed
to walk stiff-legged to the watering trough
from which the old man lifts a white lid of ice.
Twice a day he shovels ensilage into their stalls

164

and shakes hay down from the loft, stuffing a forkful
under each steaming nose.
                              In late winter,
one after one, the pink-white udders
dry out as new calves swell their mothers' bellies.
Now these vessels of hugeness bear, one after one,
skinny-limbed small Holsteins eager to suck
the bounty of freshening. Now he climbs to the barn
in boots and overalls, two sweaters,
a cloth cap, and somebody's old woolen coat;
now he parts the calf from its mother after feeding,
and strips the udder clean,
to rejoice in the sweet frothing tonnage of milk.

          ⸙   ⸙   ⸙

Now in April, when snow remains on the north side
of boulders and sugarmaples, and green
starts from wet earth in open places the sun touches,
he unchains the cows one morning after milking
and lopes past them to open the pasture gate.
Now he returns whooping and slapping their buttocks
to set them to pasture again, and they are free
to wander eating all day long. Now these wallowing
big-eyed calf-makers, bone-rafters for leather,
awkward arks, cud-chewing lethargic mooers,
roll their enormous heads, trot, gallop, bounce,
cavort, stretch, leap, and bellow —
as if everything heavy and cold vanished at once
and cow spirits floated
weightless as clouds in the great day's windy April.

          ⸙   ⸙   ⸙

When his neighbor discovers him at eighty-seven, his head
leans into the side of his last Holstein;
she has kicked the milkpail over, and blue milk drains
through floorboards onto the manure pile in the great day.

THE HENYARD ROUND

1

From the dark yard by the sheepbarn the cock crowed
to the sun's pale
spectral foreblossoming eastward in June,
crowed,
      and crowed,
later each day through fall and winter, conquistador
of January drifts, almost useless vain strutter
with wild monomaniac eye, burnished swollen chest,
yellow feet serpent-scaled, and bloodred comb,
who mounted with a mighty flutter
his busy hens: Generalissimo Rooster
of nobody's army.
           When he was old we cut his head off
on the sheepyard choppingblock, watching his drummajor
prance, his last resplendent march.
As I saw him diminish, as we plucked each feathery badge,
cut off his legs, gutted him,
and boiled him three hours for our fricassee Sunday
dinner, I understood
How the Mighty Are Fallen, and my great-uncle Luther,
who remembered the Civil War,
risen from rest after his morning's sermon, asked
God's blessing on our food.

2

At the depot in April, parcel post went cheep-cheep
in rectangular cardboard boxes, each
trembling with fifty chicks. When we opened
the carton in the cool toolshed
fifty downed fluffers cheep-cheeping
rolled and teetered.
           All summer it was my chore

to feed them, to water them.
Twice a day I emptied a fouled pan
and freshened it from the trough; twice a day
I trudged up hill to the grainshed, filled
sapbuckets at wooden tubs and poured
grain into v-shaped feeders, watching the greedy
fluster and shove.
                    One summer
I nursed a blind chick six weeks — pale yellow,
frail, tentative, meek,
who never ate except when I gapped space for her.
I watched her grow little by little,
but every day outpaced
by the healthy beaks that seized feed
to grow monstrous — and one morning
discovered her dead: meatless, incorrigible.

   3
At summer's end the small roosters departed
by truck, squawking. Pullets
moved to the henhouse and extruded each day
new eggs, harvested morning and night. Hens roosted
in darkness locked from skunk and fox,
and let out at dawn footed the brittle yard,
tilting on stiff legs to peck the corncobs
clean; to gobble turnip peels, carrot tops, even
the shells of yesterday's eggs. Hens labored
to fill eggboxes the eggman shipped
to Boston, and to provide our breakfast, gathered
at the square table.
                    When the eggmaking frenzy
ceased, when each in her own time set
for weeks as if setting itself made eggs,
each used-up, diligent hen
danced on the packed soil of the henyard her final
headless jig, and boiled

in her pale shape
                    featherless as an egg, consumed
like the blind chick, like Nannie,
who died one summer at seventy-seven, childish,
deaf, unable to feed herself, demented . . .

WHIP-POOR-WILL

As the last light
of June withdraws
the whip-poor-will sings
his clear brief notes
by the darkening house, then
rises abruptly from sandy
ground, a brown bird
in the near-night, soaring
over shed and woodshed
to far dark fields. When
he returns at dawn,
in my sleep I hear
his three syllables make
a man's name, who slept
fifty years in this bed
and ploughed these fields:
Wes-ley-Wells . . . *Wes-*
ley-Wells . . .
                    It is good
to wake early in high
summer with work to do,
and look out the window
at a ghost bird lifting away
to drowse all morning
in his grassy hut.

NEW ANIMALS

Waking one morning
we cannot find
Kate or Wesley,
or his cows and sheep,
or the hens she looks
after. In my dream
we spend all morning
looking for their old
bodies in tall grass
beside barn
and henyard. Finally
we discover them,
marching up the dirt
road from Andover —
excited, laughing, waving
to catch our attention
as they shepherd
new animals
home to the farm.
They traded Holsteins
and Rhode Island Reds
for zebras, giraffes,
apes, and tigers. They lead
their parade back
to the barn, and the sheep-
dog ostrich
nips at the errant
elephant's heels
and goads the gaudy
heroic lions
and peacocks that keen
AIEE AIEE.

THE ROCKER

"He played jacks with me
after Sunday School,
such a big, gentle boy.
I was ten years
old." The worn-flat
rockers of her chair
bump on the kitchen
floor. "That night they
couldn't find him.
With lanterns the men
climbed the hill
by his mother's house
to look for him; called
his name and stood
listening. Then
their lanterns turned
the windows yellow, one
by one. They told how,
when they climbed up
the attic stairs,
Alexander Blackmore's
nose bumped
into boots swinging."
She's down to eighty
pounds, same as her age,
and her shiny white
fists grip
the rocker's arms.
"He pushed them off
and the boots swung
back and hit him."
Her kettle steams;
her fat old tomcat

turns his head
when a mouse skitters
over linoleum.

TWELVE SEASONS

Snow starts at twilight. All night the house
trembles as ploughs thrust up and down
the highway. Snow keeps on falling — willy-nilly,
irresponsible, letting the wind do its work, gathering
rounded in drifts. Morning flakes
and densens. Overspread by gray and lucid snow,
we sit beside iron stoves
and kettles that steam dry air. At midnight clouds
withdraw, and the full moon relumes
the soft sculpted bowl of this valley.
In the unspotted stillness, in luminous gray shade,
the child's cry opens like a knife blade.

Old weathered elm chunks, birch still sappy,
oak, maple, ash: irregular slabs of August sun,
ripped from the hill, stacked in the woodshed
with difficulty; — this rummage of slivers, this sprain
of fists, this toe fracture . . . At bedtime we pile
three split oak logs high in the iron stove.
At six when we open drafts and door in the unbreathing
room, struts of wood unpack in the stove's hollow,
July's green steeple and the acorn tree
dismantle before us, and the sun made solid
transforms into golden heat — like a gift
from August carried by starlight over winter dunes.

Hook a six-pound slab of pale brisket from the barrel's
brine. Bring it to a boil in a great kettle
and pour off the flaky water. Boil it again
four hours and a half. Spiral the peel
from a dense yellow turnip and cleaver it
into eight wedges; drop in the pot for the last
hour's boiling. Ten minutes later put the potatoes in,
scrubbed in their jackets. With half an hour left,
add carrots and the Turkish domes of onions.
For the last twelve minutes lay chunks of cabbage,
green-white and quavering, on the erupting surface
of the inexhaustible pot over the assembling fire.

A doe walks in the railroad's trench on corrupt snow.
Her small hooves poke holes in the crust,
melted and frozen again, that scrapes her ankles
as her starved head swivels for bark. So the dogpack,
loosened one by one from stove-warm houses, gathers
seven leaping bodies that larrup, sliding
along the crust, like twelve-year-old boys at recess
chasing a sissy. They rip her throat out.
Walking on a mild day, as snow melts from the tracks,
we find the body hollowed by birds and coyotes
and drag it aside, into a grove of yellow birch
that beaver forested, leaving spiky stumps behind.

One braid of smoke lifts and undoes itself
over the clapboard cottage of Martha Bates Dudley
all year, keeping nine decades warm in housedress,
slippers, sweater, cardigan, and shawl
as she sits in the tall rocker knitting,
tatting, and crocheting for the fancywork table
at the Church Fair, the first Saturday in August.
Charity occupies a house emptied of talkative dead;
charity occupies a body turned witness of small pains.
When she adds a stick of maple every hour

to her white Glenwood, soup rolls its knuckles
of bubble and froth and works all day without stopping.

Sharpen the scythe with a blue whetstone, wrist
snapping from edge to edge as quick as a hummingbird.
Mow keeping heel to ground or the blade's point
will catch earth; keep feet apart, rocking,
leaning forward; use the steel's weight like a spring
to pull the body forward; sweep back and forth
in a long arc of swaths, in broad semicircles;
march into the wavering field of millet
leaving a swooped line behind you, the mower's
flattened crescents that your ancestors made before you
when they entered Canaan
to husband their land with thighs, shoulders, and forearms.

After supper Belle goes fishing with her uncle Sherman
in his leaky rowboat, in summer twilight
outlined by gnats. They catch the long silver-pencil
pickerel when they are lucky; suckers, horned pout.
Sherman and Belle dream in their trim-painted boat
of fish dozing in black sleepy water,
and sit in the half-light on motionless water,
alone except for Benjamin Eckersley,
cross-pond in his rowboat, under the faint haze of his pipe.
Whatever they look at speaks to them — the water
in watery speech, birch in the language of birches.
They drift in the boat of their affection.

After two weeks of heat pressing on sweetcorn —
haze dropping on hay, opaque air — this morning wakes
cool with a bright wind, and the mountain
clear, Kearsarge blue under transparent
running air, cold rapid energy sharp as pitchforks.
It is a morning for fires in the stove,
wood's architecture opening shafts and corridors of fire,

vacancies, gases. It is a day for clearing
rocks from the fields, volunteers, elm saplings.
Tomorrow we eat the body and drink the blood
in the community of the white church
where the day's pleasure occupies a pew beside suffering.

She works uphill over the ankle-turning stones
of New Canada Road, under yellow birch leaves that start
from ghost trunks. Pausing for breath, she gazes
west into Vermont past bright swampmaples, then climbs
past overgrown appletrees in a double row —
pocked fruit for deer. She finds the gap in the wall
and enters the clearing where a granite doorstep
opens to a cellarhole, shingles collapsed in weed.
Behind the dead elm with its branch for swinging from,
beside the big rock where they played church,
in the stove-in playhouse their father built for them
seventy years ago, her cold sister makes tea.

Now wind rises, and great yellow man-shaped leaves
turn chill air solid, turn air raucous
with leaves calling, calling as each gust starts
a thousand divers and dancers through beaded cold
to their common grave on whitening grass.
Ghosts rise, ghosts whirl in the afternoon leaves,
as the dead visit the declining year. We take them in,
and west of the pond, where the eagle kept house,
yellow light swoops down, turning low hills black
under pale blue that fades into violet; south,
half-dark half-light Kearsarge rises
blinking a cautionary red beam every forty seconds.

At eighty-two, Andy Hunt sits by the stove's fire
he built in morning solitude to warm old bones.
Last summer when he dug worms from fibrous earth
by the woodshed's eighteen-sixty-five oak sill,

174

he found this oblong rusted box under a foot of dirt,
with two hundred clay marbles in it — pitted, irregular
greens, pinks, and blues. Andy sits by the stove
and picks the marbles over: — these petrified
flowers of an unrecognizable summer, gathered
by some dead boy, he doesn't know who,
hidden he doesn't know why or when,
and never redeemed unless he redeems them now.

December sun marks cold edges of Kearsarge
and stiff upright cornstalks, gray small trunks
casting shadows hard as maple splinters.
Now the woodchuck sleeps curled in his burrow;
skunk and raccoon are sleeping; snakes
doze in their holes, and bears in shallow recesses.
Now we gather in black evening, in Advent,
as our nervous and reasonable fingers continually reach
for the intangible. Now we wait together;
we add wood to the castiron stove, and midnight's
candlelight trembles on the ceiling
as we drowse waiting. Someone is at the door.

SCENIC VIEW

Every year the mountains
get paler and more distant —
trees less green, rock piles
disappearing — as emulsion
from a billion Kodaks
sucks color out.
In fifteen years
Monadnock and Kearsarge,

the Green Mountains
and the White, will turn
invisible, all
tint removed
atom by atom to albums
in Medford and Greenwich,
while over the valleys
the still intractable granite
rears with unseeable peaks
fatal to airplanes.

SUMS

from *The Daye-Boke of Adam Raison,*
1515–1560

From that daye thee Hart strokys
his meeter. Kingesguard sette us
at Rodesyde while they stepd himm
past us in his whyte Veste:
Necke stode free of its Collare
for thee Axe at thee 8e Belle.

Somme theyre cryed: "Kingeslayer
Piggeshart!" Boyes through Turdes
striking his Bodye striding —
his Feete wide to balance himm,
his Handes thongedd thigither —
the laste Rodd of his Manhode.

In his Necke a blew Veyne throbbd
thee Hartsblodde — *onne,* and *onne* —
as if to rekkon Summes. Then Knees

bangd on Wode of Scaffholde,
Axemann gruntyd, glintt of bryght
Blade. Blodde-russhe.

THE REVOLUTION

In the Great Hall where Lady Ann by firelight after dining alone
nodded and dreamed that her cousin Rathwell turned into a unicorn,
and woke shuddering, and was helped to her chambers, undressed,
and looked after, and in the morning arose to read Mrs. Hemans,
sitting prettily on a garden bench, with no sound disturbing
her whorled ear but the wind and the wind's apples falling,
                    the servants

tended fires, answered bells, plucked grouse, rolled sward, fetched
eggs, clipped hedge, mended linen, baked scones, and served tea.
While Lady Ann grew pale playing the piano, and lay late in bed aging,
she regretted Rathwell who ran off to Ceylon with his indescribable
desires, and vanished — leaving her to the servants who poached, larked,
drank up the cellar, emigrated without notice, copulated, conceived,
                    and begot us.

OLD TIMERS' DAY

When the tall puffy
figure wearing number
nine starts
late for the fly ball,

laboring forward
like a lame truckhorse
startled by a gartersnake,
— this old fellow
whose body we remember
as sleek and nervous
as a filly's —

and barely catches it
in his glove's
tip, we rise
and applaud weeping:
On a green field
we observe the ruin
of even the bravest
body, as Odysseus
wept to glimpse
among shades the shadow
of Achilles.

THE BASEBALL PLAYERS

Against the bright
grass the white-knickered
players tense, seize,
and attend. A moment
ago, outfielders
and infielders adjusted
their clothing, glanced
at the sun and settled
forward, hands on knees;
the pitcher walked back

of the hill, established
his cap and returned;
the catcher twitched
a forefinger; the batter
rotated his bat
in a slow circle. But now
they pause: wary,
exact, suspended —
                    while
abiding moonrise
lightens the angel
of the overgrown
garden, and Walter Blake
Adams, who died at
fourteen, waits
under the footbridge.

GRANITE AND GRASS

I

On Ragged Mountain birches twist from rifts in granite.
Great ledges show gray through sugarbush. Brown bears
doze all winter under granite outcroppings or in cellarholes
the first settlers walled with fieldstone.
Granite markers recline in high abandoned graveyards.

Although split by frost or dynamite, granite is unaltered;
earthquakes tumble boulders across meadows; glaciers
carry pebbles with them as they grind south
and melt north, scooping lakes for the Penacook's trout.
Stone bulks, reflects sunlight, bears snow, and persists.

When highway-makers cut through a granite hill, scoring
deep trench-sides with vertical drillings, they leave behind
glittering sculptures, monuments to the granite state
of nature, emblems of permanence
that we worship in daily disease, and discover in stone.

2

But when we climb Ragged Mountain past cordwood stumpage,
over rocks of a dry creekbed, in company of young hemlock,
only granite remains unkind. Uprising in summer, in woods
and high pastures, our sister the fern breathes, trembles,
and alters, delicate fronds outspread and separate.

The fox pausing for scent cuts holes in hoarfrost.
Quail scream in the fisher's jaw; then the fisher dotes.
The coy-dog howls, raising puppies that breed more puppies
to rip the throats of rickety deer in March.
The moose's antlers extend, defending his wife for a season.

Mother-and-father grass lifts in the forsaken meadow,
grows tall under sun and rain, uncut, turns yellow,
sheds seeds, and under assault of snow relents; in May
green generates again. When the bear dies, bees construct
honey from nectar of cinquefoil growing through rib bones.

3

Ragged Mountain was granite before Adam divided.
Grass lives because it dies. If weary of discord
we gaze heavenward through the same eye that looks at us,
vision makes light of contradiction:
Granite is grass in the holy meadow of the soul's repose.

A SISTER ON THE TRACKS

Between pond and sheepbarn, by maples and watery birches,
Rebecca paces a double line of rust
in a sandy trench, striding on black
creosoted eight-by-eights.
                              In nineteen-forty-three,
wartrains skidded tanks,
airframes, dynamos, searchlights, and troops
to Montreal. She counted cars
from the stopped hayrack at the endless crossing:
ninety-nine, one hundred; and her grandfather Ben's
voice shaking with rage and oratory told
how the mighty Boston and Maine
kept the Statehouse in its pocket.
                              Today Rebecca walks
a line that vanishes, in solitude
bypassed by wars and commerce. She remembers the story
of the bunting'd day her great-great-great-
grandmother watched the first train roll and smoke
from Potter Place to Gale
with fireworks, cider, and speeches. Then the long rail
drove west, buzzing and humming; the hive of rolling stock
extended a thousand-car'd perspective
from Ohio to Oregon, where men who left stone farms
rode rails toward gold.
                              On this blue day she walks
under a high jet's glint of swooped aluminum pulling
its feathery contrail westward. She sees ahead
how the jet dies into junk, and highway wastes
like railroad. Beside her the old creation retires,
hayrack sunk like a rowboat
under its fields of hay. She closes her eyes
to glimpse the vertical track that rises
from the underworld of graves,

soul's ascension connecting dead to unborn, rails
that hum with a hymn of continual vanishing
where tracks cross.
              For she opens her eyes to read
on a solitary gravestone next to the rails
the familiar names of Ruth and Matthew Bott, born
in a Norfolk parish, who ventured
the immigrant's passionate Exodus westward to labor
on their own land. Here love builds
its mortal house, where today's wind carries
a double scent of heaven and cut hay.

A SISTER BY THE POND

I

An old *Life* photograph
prints itself on Rebecca's mind: The German
regular army hangs
partisans on the Russian front.
Grandfather Wehrmacht in his tight-
collared greatcoat adjusts
the boy's noose as his elderly
adjutant watches. Beside the boy,
his girl companion has already
strangled, her gullet cinched when a soldier
kicked the box from her feet.
In the photograph, taken
near Minsk, gray sky behind him
the summer of nineteen-forty-one,
the boy smiles —
as if he understood that being hanged
is no great matter.

2

At this open winter's end, in the wrack
and melt of April,
Rebecca walks on the shore by her summer
swimming place, by Eagle Pond
where the ice rots. Over
the pocked glaze, puddles of gray stain
spread at mid-day. Every year
an ice-fisherman waits one weekend
too many, and his shack drowns
among reeds and rowboats. She counts
the season's other
waste: mostly the beaver's work — stout
trees chewed through, stripped
of bark, trailing
twigs in the water. Come summer,
she will drag away the trash, and loll on red
blossoms of moss.

3

She walks on the shore today
by "Sabine," the beach her young
aunts made, where they loafed together,
hot afternoons of the war. She arranged
freshwater mussels on moss;
watched a mother duck
lead her column; studied the quick
repose of minnows; lying on pine needles loosened
out of her body. Forty years
later Rebecca walks
by the same water: When July's lilies
open in the cove
by the boggy place where bullfrogs
bellow, they gather the sun
as they did when she picked a bunch
for her grandfather Ben
in his vigorous middle age.

4

In October she came here last,
strolling by pondside with her daughter,
whose red hair brightened
against black-green fir.
Rebecca gazed at her daughter's pale
watery profile, admiring the forehead broad
and clear like Ben's, without guile,
and took pleasure in the affection
of her silent company. By the shore
a maple stood upright,
casting red leaves, its trunk gnawed
to a three-inch waist
of centerwood that bore the branches'
weight. Today when she looks for it, it
is eaten all the way down; blond splinters
show within the gray
surface of the old chewing.

5

Two weeks ago she drove her daughter
to the Hematology Clinic
of the Peter Bent Brigham Hospital
and paced three hours
among bald young women and skeletal boys
until a resident spoke
the jargon of reassurance. By the felled
maple Rebecca's heart
sinks like the fisherman's shack. She sees again
her son's long body twist
in the crushed Fiesta: A blue light revolves
at three in the morning; white-coated helpers
lift him onto a stretcher;
the pulverized windshield glitters
on black macadam
and in the abrasions of his face.

6

In the smile of the boy hanged
near Minsk, and in the familiar entropy
of April at Eagle Pond,
she glimpses ahead a winter
of skeleton horses in electric snow.
That April, only the deep burrow-hiders
will emerge who slept
below breath and nightmare: Blacksnake,
frog, and woodchuck
take up their customs among milkweed
that rises through bones
of combines. That summer, when blackberries
twist from the cinders
of white houses, the bear
will pick at the unripe fruit
as he wastes and grows thin, fur
dropping off in patches from his gray skin.

7

Today, at the pond's edge, old
life warms from the suspense of winter.
Pickerel hover under the pitted, corrupt
surface of April ice
that erodes at the muddy shoreline
where peepers will sing
and snapping turtles bury their eggs.
She sways in the moment's trembling
skin and surge: She desires only
repose, wishing to rise
as the fire wishes or to sink
with the wish and nature of stones.
She wants her soul to loosen
from its body, to lift into sky
as a bird or withdraw as a fish into water
or into water itself
or into weeds that waver in water.

THE DAY I WAS OLDER

The Clock
The clock on the parlor wall, stout as a mariner's clock,
disperses the day. All night it tolls the half-hour
and the hour's number with resolute measure,
approaching the poles and crossing the equator
over fathoms of sleep. Warm
in the dark next to your breathing,
below the thousand favored stars, I feel
horns of gray water heave
underneath us, and the ship's pistons
pound as the voyage continues over the limited sea.

The News
After tending the fire, making coffee, and pouring milk
for cats, I sit in a blue chair each morning,
reading obituaries in the Boston *Globe*
for the mean age; today there is MANUFACTURER CONCORD 53,
EX-CONGRESSMAN SAUGUS 80 — and I read
that Emily Farr is dead, after a long illness in Oregon.
Once in an old house we talked for an hour, while a coal fire
brightened in November twilight and wavered
our shadows high on the wall
until our eyes fixed on each other. Thirty years ago.

The Pond
We lie by the pond on a late August afternoon
as a breeze from low hills in the west stiffens water
and agitates birch leaves yellowing above us.
You set down your book
and lift your eyes to white trunks tilting from shore.
A mink scuds through ferns; an acorn tumbles.
Soon we will turn to our daily business.
You do not know that I am watching, taking pleasure

in your breasts that rise and fall as you breathe.
Then I see mourners gathered by an open grave.

The Day
Last night at suppertime I outlived my father, enduring
the year, month, day, hour, and moment
when he lay back on a hospital bed in the guest room
among cylinders of oxygen — mouth open, nostrils and pale
blue lips fixed unquivering. Father of my name,
father of long fingers, I remember your dark hair
and your face almost unwrinkled. Now I have waked
more mornings to frost whitening the grass,
read the newspaper more times, and stood more times,
my hand on a doorknob without opening the door.

The Cup
From the Studebaker's backseat, on our Sunday drives,
I watched her earrings sway. Then I walked uphill
beside an old man carrying buckets
under birches on an August day. Striding at noontime,
I looked at wheat and at river cities. In the crib
my daughter sighed opening her eyes. I kissed the cheek
of my father dying. By the pond an acorn fell.
You listening here, you reading these words as I write them,
I offer this cup to you: Though we drink
from this cup every day, we will never drink it dry.

ACORNS

An oak twig drops
in the path as we climb
the slippery needled
slope from the pond: nine

flame-shaped leaves,
glossy, with yellow-
green sinews veering
out from red spines;

under the leaves, two
acorns depart
from woody cups:
shiny, metallic,

verdant, as acorn-
meat presses from
inside out, volume
thrusting to smooth

the tumid surface
of tiny mast-woman
breasts, nipple-
points centering pale

aureoles. We climb
slowly, carrying
a wicker basket up
the slippery path.

FOR AN EXCHANGE
OF RINGS

They rise into mind,
the young lovers
of eighteen-nineteen:
As they walk together

in a walled garden
of Hampstead, tremulous,
their breathing quick,
color high, eyes lucent,
he places the floral
ring with its almondine
stone on her finger.
Although in two winters,
hopeless in Rome,
her letters unopened
beside him, he will
sweat, cough, and die;
although forty years
later a small old
woman will wear
his ring and locket
of hair as she stops
breathing — now, in
Hampstead, in eighteen-
nineteen, they are
wholly indifferent
to other days as they
moisten and swell.

THE IMPOSSIBLE MARRIAGE

The bride disappears. After twenty minutes of searching
we discover her in the cellar, vanishing against a pillar
in her white gown and her skin's original pallor.
When we guide her back to the altar, we find the groom
in his slouch hat, open shirt, and untended beard
withdrawn to the belltower with the healthy young sexton

from whose comradeship we detach him with difficulty.
O never in all the meetinghouses and academies
of compulsory Democracy and free-thinking Calvinism
will these poets marry! — O pale, passionate
anchoret of Amherst! O reticent kosmos of Brooklyn!

MR. WAKEVILLE ON INTERSTATE 90

"Now I will abandon the route of my life
as my shadowy wives abandon me, taking my children.
I will stop somewhere. I will park in a summer street
where the days tick like metal in the stillness.
I will rent the room over Bert's Modern Barbershop
where the TO LET sign leans in the plateglass window;
or I will buy the brown BUNGALOW FOR SALE.

"I will work forty hours a week clerking at the paintstore.
On Fridays I will cash my paycheck at Six Rivers Bank
and stop at Harvey's Market and talk with Harvey.
Walking on Maple Street I will speak to everyone.
At basketball games I will cheer for my neighbors' sons.
I will watch my neighbors' daughters grow up, marry,
raise children. The joints of my fingers will stiffen.

"There will be no room inside me for other places.
I will attend funerals regularly and weddings.
I will chat with the mailman when he comes on Saturdays.
I will shake my head when I hear of the florist
who drops dead in the greenhouse over a flat of pansies;
I spoke with her only yesterday.
When lawyer elopes with babysitter I will shake my head.

"When Harvey's boy enlists in the Navy
I will wave goodbye at the Trailways depot with the others.
I will vote Democratic; I will vote Republican.
I will applaud the valedictorian at graduation
and wish her well as she goes away to the university
and weep as she goes away. I will live in a steady joy;
I will exult in the ecstasy of my concealment."

MY FRIEND FELIX

"Beginning at five o'clock, just before dawn rises
in the rearview mirror, I drive at eighty, alone,
all day through Texas. I am a pencil extending
a ruler's line to the unchangeable horizon
west as I repeat a thousand quarrels with my wives.
My grip on the steering wheel slackens; my mind's voice turns
mild and persuasive, quietly addressing the young
doctor at the detox center . . . but I cannot stop
hearing again, word-for-word, last winter's two o'clock
call from a motel in Albany — she would not say
where she was — as my daughter wept, sighed, begged forgiveness,
and allowed the telephone to drop from her fingers.
When I have driven straight through daylight, five-foot neon
letters rise crimson in the pale west: BAR. Thirty years
drown: I am a young man again driving with Felix
from New Haven to San Diego where he will join
his Crusader and his carrier, and in two months
overshoot the runway and slide to the Pacific's
silt bottom without jettisoning his canopy,
while a helicopter hovers an hour above him.
For a moment Felix sits alongside me again,
a young man forever, with his skin wrinkled and puffed

from thirty years of soaking in his watery chair:
All day we drove west on a ruled highway: At a BAR
we swallowed two pitchers, and back on the road again
I pulled out to pass a tractor-trailer. Another
approached and neither truck would give way; I labored past
the semi inch-by-inch and at the last half-second
sideslipped in front. As our pulses slowed we stared ahead,
and from the slipcovered seat beside me Felix spoke:
'The time that we lose, by stopping to drink, we make up
by drunken driving.' Continuing straight west I dream
of my lucky friend Felix the singlewing halfback."

MERLE BASCOM'S .22

"I was twelve when my father gave me this .22
Mossberg carbine — hand-made, with a short octagonal
barrel, stylish as an Indianfighter posing
for a photograph. We ripped up Bokar coffeecans
set into the sandbank by the track — competitive
and companionable. He was a good shot, although
his hands already trembled. Or I walked with my friend
Paul who loved airplanes and wanted to be a pilot,
and carried my rifle loosely, pointing it downward;
I aimed at squirrels and missed. Later I shot woodchucks
that ate my widowed mother's peas and Kentucky
Wonders when I visited on weekends from college,
or drove up from my Boston suburb, finding the gun
in its closet behind the woodstove. Ten years ago
my mother died; I sold up, and moved here with my work
and my second wife, gladly taking my tenancy
in the farmhouse where I intended to live and die.
I used my rifle on another generation

of woodchucks that ate our beans. One autumn an old friend
from college stayed with us after a nervous breakdown:
trembling from electroshock, depressed, suicidal.
I wrapped the octagonal Mossberg in a burlap
bag and concealed it under boards in the old grainshed.
In our quiet house he strengthened and stopped shaking.
When he went home I neglected to retrieve my gun,
and the next summer woodchucks took over the garden.
I let them. Our lives fitted mountain, creek, and hayfield.
Long days like minnows in the pond quickened and were still.
When I looked up from Plutarch another year had passed.
One Sunday the choir at our church sang Whittier's hymn
ending with 'the still small voice of calm.' Idly I thought,
'I must ask them to sing that hymn at my funeral.'
Soon after, I looked for the .22 in the shed,
half expecting it to have vanished, but finding it
wrapped intact where I left it, hardly rusted. I spent
a long evening taking it apart and cleaning it;
I thought of my father's hands shaking as he aimed it.
Then I restored the Mossberg to its accustomed place
in the closet behind the stove. At about this time
I learned that my daughter-in-law was two months pregnant:
It would be the first grandchild. One day I was walking
alone and imagined a granddaughter visiting:
She loved the old place; she swam in the summer pond with us;
she walked with us in red October; she grew older, she fell
in love with a neighbor, she married. As I daydreamed,
suddenly I was seized by a fit of revulsion:
I thought: 'Must I go through all that again? Must I live
another twenty years?' It was as if a body
rose from a hole where I had buried it years ago
while my first marriage was twisting and thrashing to death.
One night I was drunk and lost control of my Beetle
off 128 near my ranchhouse. I missed a curve
at seventy miles an hour and careered toward a stone wall.
In a hundredth of a second I knew I would die;

and, as joy fired through my body, I knew something else.
But the car slowed itself on rocks and settled to rest
between an elm and a maple; I sat breathing,
feeling the joy leach out, leaving behind the torment
and terror of my desire. Now I felt this affliction
descend again and metastasize through my body.
Today I drove ninety miles, slowly, seatbelt fastened,
to North Andover and Paul's house, where he lives flying
out of Logan for United. I asked him to hide
the firing pin of an octagonal .22.
He nodded and took it from my hands without speaking.
I cannot throw it away; it was my father's gift."

1987–1990

———————

"When I heard Monica's
        voice on the telephone, I
knew what had happened. She
        spoke almost coldly, holding
the tears or hysteria back.
        Sam had pecked her goodbye
in bed that morning the way
        he usually did;
when she got up, she assumed
        he'd left for the office
on schedule until she
        looked out and saw the Buick
parked in the carport. Sam sat
        upright in the driver's
seat with his eyes open.

        "Because I am sixty, I have
lost many friends (my mother
        who lived to be eighty-
seven looked at newspapers
        in her last years only
to read the obituaries)
        — but not friends like Sam:
We met at boarding school, roomed
        together in college,
and were best man at each
        other's weddings. It started
when we were new at Holderness,
        homesick and lonesome
as we watched the returning
        boys greeting each other
after their summers on the Cape.
        We took walks, we talked.

Our friendship endured college,
        political quarrels,
one drunken fistfight, dating
        each other's ex-girlfriends,
hitchhiking, graduation,
        and marriage; and survived
although Sam left the East
        to settle in Chicago
and drudge for a conglomerate's
        legal department,
pleading in court to deny
        workmen's compensation.
I write for the Boston *Globe*,
        considered liberal,
and whenever we met Sam
        started right in on me
for the naiveté
        of my politics. Sometimes
we argued all night long . . .
        but I learned: If I refused
to fight, one night at the end
        of our visit, after
our wives had gone to bed
        and we drank one last bourbon
together, Sammy
        would confess that he hated what
he did — work, boss, and company.
        He wanted to quit;
and he *would,* too, as soon
        as he found another job.
One night he wept
        as he told a confusing story
about a man in Florida,
        paralyzed for life
when a fork-lift crushed
        his spinal cord, who was accused

of being drunk on the job,
        which he wasn't. When Sam's
department won its case,
        Sam got a bonus. Of course
he never quit his job
        and his salary to work
for Cesar Chavez or sail
        his boat around the world.
He spent ten years planning
        early retirement and died
six weeks before retiring.

        "Sam was a good father
and loyal husband most
        of the time; in private life
he was affectionate
        and loyal; many people
virtuous in public
        privately abuse their wives
and children. Then I think:
        'What about the night-watchman,
paralyzed and cheated?
        What about *his* family?'
Then I stop thinking.

        "Sam wrote letters rarely. We met
every couple of years, here
        or there, and he called up
impulsively. Last August
        Sam and Monica drove
to our place. He looked good
        although he wheezed a little.
He referred to someone
        by name, as if I should know
who she was, and shook his head
        sharply, two or three times,

insisting: 'It was only
    an infatuation.'
One night after dinner,
    neither of us drinking much
these days, he took his guitar
    from the trunk of the car
so that we could sing old
    songs and reminisce. On Labor
Day they headed back.

    "After Monica's call I dreamed
about Sam all night. Today
    I am ten thousand times
more alive in the rearward
    vision of memory
than I am editing stories
    by recent college
graduates or typing
    'graphs on a green terminal.
I lean back, closing my eyes,
    and my sore mind repeats
home movies of one day:

    "It's October, a Sunday
in nineteen-forty-four,
    Indian summer bright with
New Hampshire leaves: Sammy
    and I walk (happy in our
new friendship, sixteen and
    seventeen years old) under
tall sugarmaples
    extravagantly Chinese red,
and russet elms still thriving,
    enormous and noble
in the blue air.
    We talk about the war going on

overseas and whether we
     will fight in it; we talk
about what we will do
     after the war and college.
I admit: I want to write novels.
     Sam thinks maybe
he could be a musician
     (he plays guitar and sings
Josh White songs) 'but maybe
     it would be better to do
something that *helps* people . . .'
     Maybe he should think about
law school? (I understand:
     He feels that his rich father
leads a fatuous life
     with his Scotch and his girlfriends.)
Although we talk excitedly,
     although we mean what
we say and listen closely
     to each other, the real
burden of our talk
     is the affection that contains
and exalts us. As it turns dark,
     we head back toward school
on a shadowy gravel road;
     we are astonished
to see ahead (on a lane
     without cars in nineteen-
forty-four, as if an apparition
     conjured there
to conclude this day that fixed
     our friendship forever)
a small table with a pitcher
     on it, three glasses,
and a sign: CIDER 5¢
     A GLASS. A screendoor swings

open on the gray unpainted
       porch of a farmhouse,
and a woman (old, fat,
       and strong) walks down the dirt path
to pour us our cider.
       She takes our nickels and sells
us a second glass and then
       gives us a third. All day
today I keep tasting
       that Sunday's almost painful
detonation of cider sweet
       and harsh in my mouth."

EDWARD'S ANECDOTE

"Late one night she told me.
       We'd come home from a party
where she drank more wine
       than usual, from nervousness

"I suppose. I was astonished,
       which is typical,
and her lover of course
       was my friend. My naiveté

"served their purposes: What
       you don't know beats your head in.
After weeping for an hour or so
       I tried screaming.

"Then I quieted down;
       then I broke her grandmother's

teapot against the pantry brickwork,
    which helped a bit.

"She kept apologizing
    as she walked back and forth,
chainsmoking. I hated her,
    and thought how beautiful

"she looked as she paced,
    which started me weeping again.
Old puzzlements began to solve
    themselves: the errand

"that took all afternoon;
    the much-explained excursion
to stay with a college roommate
    at a hunting lodge

"without a telephone;
    and of course the wrong numbers.
Then my masochistic mind
    printed Kodacolors

"of my friend and my wife
    arranged in bed together.
When I looked out the window,
    I saw the sky going

"pale with dawn; soon the children
    would wake: Thinking of them
started me weeping again.
    I felt exhausted, and

"I wanted to sleep neither
    with her nor without her,
which made me remember:
    When I was a child we knew

"a neighbor named Mr. Jaspers —
        an ordinary
gray and agreeable
        middle-aged businessman who

"joked with the neighborhood
        children when he met us on
the street, giving us pennies,
        except for once a year

"when he got insanely drunk
        and the police took him.
One time he beat his year-old
        daughter with a broomstick,

"breaking a rib bone, and as
        she screamed she kept crawling
back to her father: Where else
        should she look for comfort?"

CARLOTTA'S CONFESSION

"My grandfather's name was Augusto,
        'ow-*goose*-toe' the way he said it.
He sailed from Sicily, Palermo
        to Newark, when he was fifteen
and not quite five feet tall.
        With American food, with the remarkable
effluents of New Haven, Connecticut,
        and the gun factory,
he stretched out to five foot one.
        At thirteen I was two inches taller

than my grandfather — Carlottina
    the Giantess — and I daydreamed
of becoming a nun. Augusto caressed us,
    teased us, screamed at us,
and praised us — as long as we went
    to Mass; I adored my grandfather
and when he died named my first child Augustus.
    Gus was eight for the divorce;
Mary who is Maria now was three
    and contented. My boyfriends
teased Gus and brought him presents;
    on weekends it was Harry's girls. I was
miserable and called it adventure.
    Devils the nuns had described
vividly for us jabbed forked tails
    into me, and for every jab I took
my revenge by destroying something else:
    I had a late abortion;
I married again — for six weeks.
    From the third grade on, Gus spent more hours
in the principal's office after school
    than he did on the playground.
I got him into Country Day at ten:
    They expelled him for fighting.
He was twelve the first time the police
    called me; at fifteen, larceny
and a year in reform school. Then
    no more school and no jobs that lasted:
Gus never finished anything
    except a joint or a pint of wine.
He never went back to a shrink
    for a second appointment. Of course
he made resolutions; there was a sweetness
    to him that broke my heart,
and my heart always broke
    with his resolutions. When he was twenty

he resolved to kill himself:
    Naturally we argued about it;
sometimes I won the arguments,
    but a week later — I made pasta
every Sunday night — he'd return
    with more reasons. Sometimes with a new
job or girl he'd drop the subject;
    then there'd be another disaster
and he'd disappear for a week.
    On a wet Sunday a month ago —
after he lost a good job
    and signed up for welfare again, and moved
in again with a girlfriend
    who chippied on him — he telephoned me
to say goodbye; he had said goodbye
    many times before but this time
he called his own bluff —
    and he failed again. The shoplifted .22
caliber target pistol left him
    in Intensive Care on his back
with his eyes open and his left
    cheek twitching every nine seconds.
They had hooked him up to a machine
    but he lay staring beyond
my fury and my love forever.
    For two weeks I sat beside him
all night while machines breathed
    for him, rasping and hissing like metal cats.
In my head I kept arguing with him:
    Now the argument ran to
pulling or not pulling the plug. What a quarrel!
    Once as I drove home
from the hospital at midnight
    for a little induced sleep before
a court session in the morning,
    my mind ran a movie, like those scenes

in pantomime that they show
        behind titles: I watched myself tiptoe
into Gus's hospital room
        in a gray light; then I glanced over
my shoulder to see that no one followed; then
        I suffocated him.
The next morning the old judge delivered
        his order; after supper,
with Maria holding me, I kissed Gus
        a last time. The head nurse turned
the switches off one by one.
        By one. Very, very slowly his heart-
beats, visible on the green monitor,
        blipped farther apart. One breath
a minute. Two minutes. Then there were none.
        Next afternoon we buried
him in the non-denominational
        (meaning Protestant) graveyard.
For three days I felt gay; then the guilt:
        Repeatedly I went over
his life from the beginning, finding
        that my errors ruined his life,
fault breeding fault breeding fault:
        selfishness, lust, cruelty, greed, malice,
laziness, pride. I married myself
        to failure, now I was failure's
widow. I tried going to church, say
        what you like, where I hadn't gone
since my first divorce: My tongue grieved
        for my grandfather's wine and wafer.
First I needed to make my confession,
        my litany of error,
and I told the young priest how I had broken
        each of the commandments
except the one that forbids us to kill.
        The moment I heard myself

speak I laughed aloud — but I didn't
    laugh with amusement: Carlotta
the mother who aborted one child
    and daydreamed strangling another.
For penance he set a Hail Mary.
    'Your sins are forgiven,' he said."

BRIEF LIVES

On a Philosopher
The world is everything that is the case.
Now stop your blubbering and wash your face.

On a Future Dean
And why does Gratt teach English? Why, because
A law school felt he could not learn the laws.
"*Hamlet*," he tells his students, "you will find,
Concerns a man who can't make up his mind.
The Tempest? . . . um . . . the one with Ariel! . . .
Are there more questions now?" But one can tell
That all his will, brains, and imagination
Are concentrated on a higher station:
He wants to be in the administration.

On a Scholar
Ascribed to earth, by bookworms tilled and ploughed,
He wore his learning lightly, like a shroud.

On an Ambitious Poet
He sought in his late work, which no one reads,
The unavailing laurel of the Swedes.

On a Teacher
Chinless and slouched, gray-faced and slack of jaw,
Here plods depressed Professor Peckinpaugh,
Whose work J. Donald Adams found "exciting."
This fitted him to teach Creative Writing.

OUR WALK IN YORKSHIRE

Sheep mutter as we pass
And drop their Roman heads
Down into autumn grass
Among the stone farmsteads.

Moss wrinkles on gray walls;
Crows swarm a hedge; a rose
Drops desiccated petals
On grass that walls enclose.

Her father is the leaf
Curled in the stone gutter
As she walks in her grief
By pastures where sheep mutter.

A CAROL

The warmth of cows
    That chewed on hay
And cherubim

Protected Him
    As small He lay.

Chickens and sheep
    Knew He was there
Because all night
A holy light
    Suffused the air.

Darkness was long
    And the sun brief
When the Child arose
A man of sorrows
    And friend to grief.

A GRACE

God, I know nothing, my sense is all nonsense,
And fear of You begins intelligence:
Does it end there? For sexual love, for food,
For books and birch trees I claim gratitude,
But when I grieve over the unripe dead
My grief festers, corrupted into dread,
And I know nothing. Give us our daily bread.

MAUNDY THURSDAY'S CANDLES

We speak the verses out of Mark
And Matthew in the growing dark.

When the cock crows we know the shame
Of Peter who denied God's name.

Darkly we listen to John's news
Of crowds that jeer "King of the Jews."

Luke's verses shut the last light down
With vinegar and a thorn crown,

And in bright day, up the hillside,
"They took him to be crucified."

MATERIAL

At fourteen, parked
by the depot
in the Chevy
pickup with its
motor running,
she studies flaked
B & M paint
on clapboard and
takes all edges
in — shapes of paint
flecks, dimensions;
wood-grainy, rain-
smudged, deep-textured
lumps and fadings:
Concentration
upraises things,
like bread, like grass
after warm rain.

MOON CLOCK

Like an oarless boat through midnight's watery
ghosthouse, through lumens and shallows
of shadow, under smoky light that the full moon
reflects from snowfields to ceilings, I drift
on January's tide from room to room, pausing
by the wooden clock with its pendulum that keeps
the beat like a heart certainly beating, to wait
for the pause allowing passage
to repose's shore — where all waves halt
upreared and stony as the moon's Mycenaean lions.

MATCH

Yellow fingers
lift a match to
Virginia's
shreds and edges:
Deeply I pull
smoke in, and blood
faints at the door.

My young father
coughs, gags, and wipes
his lips with pale
narrow fingers:
When he looks at
his shaking hands,
splaying them out

to gaze at them,
I understand

how much his nails
please him, with their
faint moons always
neatly pushed to
the same quarter.

PERSISTENCE OF 1937

After fifty years Amelia Earhart's Lockheed fretted with rust
still circles over the Pacific. From her skull's scrimshaw
she peers downward, looking for a lane through permanent weather
while a sixty-year-old man carves her story onto whalebone,
slowly incising the fifth grader who paces from kitchen
through living room to parlor back to kitchen, eating unbuttered
slices of Wonder Bread, listening to the Philco for bulletins
from the Navy: *After fifty years her Lockheed still circles.*

MILKERS BROKEN UP

I was sleeping in Madison, Anthony Bradbury's spare room,
after a day when we visited a gallery to look at collages
he had pasted from illustrations torn out of magazines;
we stayed up late reminiscing about twenty-five years
of friendship, about youthful marriages and grown-up children.
We knew each other first in our thirties, when we appeared
to have settled into the orderly progression of our lives
as into houses on streets lined with elms and Plymouths,
before the divorces and assassinations. In nineteen-sixty,

we met Wednesdays at the Grasshopper Tavern near Fenway,
half a dozen novelists and poets, gossiping, telling stories,
monitoring the systems by which we confirmed eminence
and notoriety. I remember eating a hamburger while Hanema
said again, "He always speaks well of *you*," and Da Silva
laughed again — as Robert Lowell slid through the door;
rapidly and furtively he drank a Bass, glanced quickly around,
and bolted. He looked like a cartoon of misery — "as *tortured*,"
Michele or somebody said, "as one of his damned linebreaks."

At Tony's I dreamed the familiar dream in which we remember
a duty neglected: I walked up and down in the farmhouse,
pacing, the way as a boy I paced, planning my life out . . .
Then I remembered: My grandfather had died a week ago
and I had forgotten to milk the cows! I ran to the pasture;
their udders had swollen and split: Covering my mouth
I saw the black-and-white milkers break up into pieces
like the roadkills crows pick at, their body parts floating
over rocky pastures, ripped meat bloody and still alive.

NOTES FOR NOBODY

I

The first time I met him Henry Moore was sixty. Before tea
— after working nine hours on maquettes, waxes, an elmwood,
and the plaster of a monumental two-part reclining figure —
he played an ardent game of ping-pong. He was quick, wiry,
resourceful, competitive, thirty years older, and I beat him.
When I smashed the ball to his backhand before he could swing
his paddle around, he swatted the ball over the net
with the flat of his left hand. I caught the ball, and Henry
looked surprised: "That *counts*," he said, "doesn't it?"

2

After I wrote a background about Moore for a *CBS Reports,*
I chatted with an intelligent television producer in London.
We talked with gathering excitement about what we would do,
until the producer remembered what counted. He laughed, shaking
his head: "Here we are, enthusiastic . . . and when we do it,
nobody will watch." When I asked him, "How many is nobody?"
he paused and his bright face blenched: "Maybe five million."

3

The last time I saw him he was eighty-six. "Henry," I said,
"I hear you've discovered the secret of life. What is it?"
So he told me: "The secret is to devote your life to one desire.
Concentrate your life on achieving this desire, *everything,*
but remember: Choose something you can't do!" Henry laughed
as he shifted his weight in the wheelchair before the coal fire
in his living room; maybe the catheter was uncomfortable.

4

He liked to repeat advice from Rodin for young sculptors:
"If you're working on a maquette, and it's not going right,
don't keep picking at the wax or the clay, making little changes:
Try dropping it on the floor; see what it looks like then!"
He remembered Rodin quoting the old craftsman who taught him
to model, when they labored together in an artisan's workshop.
"Rodin," said Adolphe Constant, "your leaves are too flat;
make some of your leaves with the tips pointing up at you.
Never consider a surface except as the extremity of a volume."

SIX NAPS IN ONE DAY

1

In the nap there are numerous doors, boudoirs, a talking hall
of sisters who gesture underwater, and bricked-up memoirs
with closets inside. There are bikes and desks in the nap,

2

corridors of glory, water, and pots of ivy hooked to ceiling
or ocean floor. Apes play with papers on the busy desk
I swim up to, through laborious sleep water. Rex the butcher

3

wears a straw hat sleeping on sawdust. When the extinguished
U-boat, flapping bat wings, settles under millennial silt,
whose eyes gleam through the periscope? They are Regina's.

4

Two squadrons of black biplanes dogfight over the trenches
of nineteen-seventeen, death's-heads graven on engine cowlings,
helmeted pilots' faces turned into skulls, and their bones

5

as shadowy blue as underwater feet in the shoestore x-ray.
The gibbon's cry hobbles on the wooded shore, like the cry
of this bed. He walks by the ocean's tide a thousand years

6

in his gown of claws and hair, a deposed king searching
for sleep's bosom and the tall queen of dunes: Regina
skulks hiding in salt grass — while the halt gibbon howls.

TOMORROW

Although the car radio warned that
"war threatened" as "Europe mobilized,"
we set out for the World's Fair on the
last day of August, nineteen-thirty-
nine. My grandparents came visiting
from New Hampshire to Connecticut
once in three years; it wasn't easy
to find somebody to milk the cows,
to feed the hens and sheep: Maybe that's
why we went ahead, with my father
driving down the new Merritt Parkway
toward Long Island. I was ten years old;
for months I had looked forward to this
trip to the Fair. Everywhere I looked
I saw the Trylon and Perisphere —
on ashtrays, billboards, and Dixie Cups;
in *Life* —: those streamlined structures that stood
for The World of Tomorrow, when Dad
would autogyro to pick up Rick
and Judy from a school so modern
it resembled an Airstream trailer.
As we drove home late at night — it was
already morning in Warsaw — I
tried not to let my eyes close. My dear
grandfather — wearing a suit instead
of overalls; my grandmother with
pearls from Newberry's — held my hand tight
in silence. Soon I would fall asleep
as we drove down the Parkway, but first
we stop-and-started through city blocks,
grave in the Pontiac heading north
toward Connecticut, past newsboys
hoarse, dark, and ragged, flapping papers
at the red lights of intersections.

TUBES

1

"Up, down, good, bad," said
the man with the tubes
up his nose, "there's lots
of variety . . .
However, notions
of balance between
extremes of fortune
are *stupid* — or at
best unobservant."
He watched as the nurse
fed pellets into
the green nozzle that
stuck from his side. "Mm,"
said the man. "Good. Yum.
(Next time more basil . . .)
When a long-desired
baby is born, what
joy! More happiness
than we find in sex,
more than we take in
success, revenge, or
wealth. But should the same
infant die, would you
measure the horror
on the same rule? Grief
weighs down the seesaw;
joy cannot budge it."

2

"When I was nineteen,
I told a thirty-
year-old man what a

218

fool I had been at
sixteen. Listening,
he looked crestfallen:
'We were always,' he
said glancing down, 'a
fool three years ago.' "

3
The man with the tubes
up his nostrils spoke
carefully: "I don't
regret what I did,
but that I claimed I
did the opposite.
If I was faithless
or treacherous and
cowardly, there was
much to fear — but I
regret that I called
myself loyal, brave,
and honorable."

4
"We are all dying
of something, always,
but our degrees of
awareness differ,"
he said offering
the vein of her choice
to the young woman
with many test tubes.
"We die of habits,
deplorable ones
like merely living:
finally fatal."

5

"Of all illusions,"
said the man with the
tubes up his nostrils,
IVs, catheter,
and feeding nozzle,
"the silliest one
was hardest to lose.
For years I supposed
that after climbing
exhaustedly up
with pitons and ropes,
I would arrive at
last on the plateau
of *Walking-level-*
forever-among-
moss-with-red-blossoms,
or the other one
of *Lolling-in-sun-*
looking-down-at-old-
valleys-I-started-
from. Of course, of course:
A continual
climbing is the one
form of arrival
we ever come to —
unless we suppose
that the wished-for height
and house of desire
is tubes up the nose."

VALLEY OF MORNING

Jack Baker
rises when
the steeple
clock strikes three
to shape dough
into pans
and wed pale
rising bread
to the fire,
trays shoved in
clay ovens
over wood
coals. After
the summer
sun touches
the church's
steeple, he
pulls from his
bakestove two
hundred loaves,
crusted brown
with damp fire
inside. Now
the valley
of morning
wakes breathing
bread's air, fresh
loaves for the
day's mouth, for
meadow, lane,
and row house.

THE COFFEE CUP

The newspaper, the coffee cup, the dog's
    impatience for his morning walk:
These fibers braid the ordinary mystery.
    After the marriage of lovers
the children came, and the schoolbus
    that stopped to pick up the children,

and the expected death of the retired
    mailman Anthony "Cat" Middleton
who drove the schoolbus for a whole
    schoolyear, a persistence enduring
forever in the soul of Marilyn,
    who was six years old that year.

We dug a hole for him. When his widow
    Florence sold the Cape and moved to town
to live near her daughter, the Mayflower
    van was substantial and unearthly.
Neither lymphoma nor a brown-and-white
    cardigan twenty years old

made an exception, not elbows nor
    Chevrolets nor hills cutting blue
shapes on blue sky, not Maple Street
    nor Main, not a pink-striped canopy
on an ice cream store, not grass.
    It was ordinary that on the day

of Cat's funeral the schoolbus arrived
    driven by a woman called Mrs. Ek,
freckled and thin, wearing a white
    bandana and overalls, with one
eye blue and the other gray. Everything
    is strange; nothing is strange:

yarn, the moon, gray hair in a bun,
New Hampshire, putting on socks.

SPEECHES

1
Two old men
meet at the lunch
counter

of Blackwater Bill's
after the first
hard

frost: "And how
did your garden
fare?"

2
"Sherm never
was afraid
of work."

3
Chester Ludlow
told me stories
about my

two great-grand-
fathers Chester
remembered,

about frogging
one hundred
  bullfrogs,

about his old
steam-tractor
  Greta

that blew up
on the Fourth
  of July —

and when I stood
to go, Chester
  asked, "You

going to write
this down
  in a book?"

"May be." "Told
you a lot
  of lies."

4
"It's down to
the store up by
  Wilmot way."

5
If you asked,
"Does it look
  like rain?"

during the year's
worst downpour,
  Kate said,

"Maybe, I guess,
perhaps, I
   suppose so . . ."

6
At Wilmot
town meeting,
   Bob the town

moderator asked,
"All those in
   favor of

buying Henry
his new front-
   loader?"

7
Wes said, "Saw
a piece about you
   in the paper."

I told him,
"Oh, I turn up
   everyplace."

"Yup," said
Wes. "Just like
   horseshit."

8
Lila dialed
Bertha to tell
   her go

look out her
parlor window
   east:

"It's as pretty
as a picture
　　postcard."

9
"Fellow lost
his bobhouse,
　　works

down to Henry's,
's he the Budd
　　boy's wife

ran off with
the bread driver
　　hates beaver?"

"Blows up dams with
TNT? No, that's
　　not him."

10
At Blackwater
Bill's, Jenny
　　yells to Claude

in the kitchen, "Hey,
Froggie, nuke us
　　some beans."

THIS POEM

1

This poem is why
I lie down at night
to sleep; it is why
I defecate, read,
and eat sandwiches;
it is why I get
up in the morning;
it is why I breathe.

2

You think (and I know
because you told me)
that poems exist
to *say* things, as you
telephone and I
write letters — as if
this poem practiced
communication.

3

One time this poem
compared itself to
new machinery,
and another time
to a Holstein's cud.
Eight times five times eight
counts three hundred and
twenty syllables.

4

When you require it,
this poem consoles —

the way a mountain
comforts by staying
as it was despite
earthquakes, Presidents,
divorces, and frosts.
Granite continues.

5

This poem informs
the hurt ear wary
of noises, and sings
to the weeping eye.
When the agony
abates itself, one
may appreciate
arbitrary art.

6

This poem is here.
Could it be someplace
else? Every question
is the wrong question.
The only answer
saunters down the page
in its broken lines
strutting and primping.

7

It styles itself not
for the small mirror
of its own regard —
nor even for yours:
to fix appearance;
to model numbers;
to name charity
"the greatest of these."

8

All night this poem
knocks at the closed door
of sleep: "Let me in."
Suppose all poems
contain this poem,
dreaming one knowledge
shaped by the measure
of the body's word.

PRAISE FOR DEATH

1

Let us praise death that turns pink cheeks to ashes,
that reduces father from son and daughter, that sets tears
in the tall widow's eye. Let us praise death that gathers
us loose-limbed and weeping by the grave's edge in the flat
yard near the sea that continues. Let us praise death

2

that fastens my body to yours and renders skin
against skin sometimes intolerably sweet, as October
sweetens the flesh of a McIntosh apple. Let us praise
death that prints snapshots, fixing an afternoon forty
years ago on a sandy lane. While we stand holding

3

each other, let us praise death as a dog praises
its master, bowing, paying obeisance, rolling over;
let us praise death as a spaniel praises a pitbull.
What remained of her at the end, compared to my friend
eight months before, was the orange peel to the orange:

4

as if the shard of fruit — once pungent and moist, now smeared
with coffeegrounds — pulsed, opened an eye, and screamed
without stopping. As we enter the passage of agony,
imagining darkness prepared underground, we recollect
Jesus who drank from the cup: "Why have you forsaken me?"

5

Praising death we sing parts with Between-the-Rivers,
with the King of Uruk, dole's aboriginal singer.
The Victorian with his imperial figleaf praises death
like the Inca, or like the first emperor of Qin
who models a deathless army in terra cotta. Let us

6

praise rictus and the involuntary release of excrement
as the *poilu* does, and Attila, and the Vestal Virgin.
We remember the terrified face behind the plexiglass mask
as Hadrian remembers Antinous. Are you rich, young,
lucky, and handsome? Are you old and unknown?

7

Are you Mesopotamian, suburbanite, Cossack, Parisian?
We praise death so much, we endow our children with it.
At seventy-eight, Henry Adams spent the summer of 1916
discussing with Brooks "the total failure of the universe,
most especially *our* country." From London he heard

8

that Harry James was dead, who "belonged to my wife's set,"
he wrote Elizabeth Cameron, "and you know how I cling
to my wife's set." Thirty years before, he discovered Clover,
still warm, her lips damp with potassium cyanide.
"All day today," he wrote, "I have been living in the '70s."

9

By the river abandoned factories tilt like gravestones.
Mills collapse behind broken windows over soil broken

to build them, where millhands wore their lives out
standing in fractured noisy stench among endless belts
and hoses steaming waste to the fish-killing river.

10

Commerce dies; and commerce raises itself elsewhere.
If we read the Boston *Globe* on a Monday, we find fixed
to the business section the part-index: *Deaths, Comics.*
The old father's dignity, as he daily and hourly rehearses
the lines of his pain, stiffens him into a tableau vivant.

11

All day he studies the script of no-desire, scrupulous
never to want what he cannot have. He controls speech,
he controls desire, and a young man's intense blue eyes
look from his face as he asks his grandniece to purchase,
at the medical supply store, rubber pants and disposable pads.

12

Let us praise death that raises itself to such power
that nothing but death exists: not breakfast nor the Long
Island Expressway, not cigarettes nor beaches at Maui,
not the Tigers nor sunrise except under the aspect
of death. Let us praise death that recedes: One day

13

we realize, an hour after waking, that for a whole hour
we have forgotten the dead, so recently gone underground,
whom we swore we would mourn from the moment we opened
our eyes. All night in sleep I watch as the sinewy, angry
body careers and hurtles in harmless air, hovering

14

like a hang glider over the western slope of Kearsarge,
fired from the Porsche that explodes, rips open, settles,
and burns while the body still twists in the air, arms
akimbo, Exxon cap departing frail skull, ponytail out
straight, until it ends against granite. Let us praise

15

death that bursts skull, lungs, spleen, liver, and heart.
Let us praise death for the piano player who quit high school
in 1921 and played *le jazz hot* through France and Italy;
who recorded with *Lud Gluskin et son Jazz* four hundred
sides of a barrelhouse left hand; who jammed with Bix

16

at Walled Lake in 1930; who tinkled foxtrots for Goldkette
and Weems, suitcase depression nights of Wilkes-Barre
and Akron; who settled down to play clubs, give lessons,
run the musician's Local, and when he died left
a thousand books behind, with the markers still in them.

17

Let us praise the death of dirt. The builder tells us
that the most effective way to preserve topsoil
is to pave it over. Petersen's farm in Hamden raised
corn, beans, and tomatoes for sale at New Haven's markets.
For a hundred years they ripened in Adams Avenue's

18

countryside among the slow cattle of dairy farms.
Now slopes extrude hairy antennae; earth conceals itself
under parking lots and the slimy, collapsing sheds
of STOP & SHOP, BROOKS, BOB'S, CALDOR, and CRAZY EDDIES.
The empire rots turning brown. Junkyards of commerce

19

slide into tar over dirt impervious to erosion, sun, wind,
and the breaking tips of green-leafed, infrangible corn.
Beside his right eye and low on his neck shiny patches of skin
blaze the removed cancer. The fifty-year-old poet and I
drink seltzer together in the Grasshopper Tavern; he rants

20

like Thersites denouncing his Greeks. Probably it won't
kill him, but toadstool up each year: *"I want"* — he looks

longingly; desire remakes his face — *"I want so much to die."*
Let us never forget to praise the deaths of animals:
The young red tomcat — long-haired, his tail like a fox's,

21

with bird feathers of fur upstarting between his toes,
who emitted a brief squeak of astonishment, like the sound
squeezed from a rubber doll, when he jumped to the floor
from a high bookcase; who rattled a doorknob trying to open
a door for himself; who, if we then opened the same door,

22

declined our absurd, well-meaning suggestion that he use it;
who bounced and never walked; who moused assiduously
and lacking mice ripped out carpet pads for swatting;
who spent most waking hours birdwatching from the pantry
window; who sprawled upside down in our arms, splaying

23

long legs stiffly out, great ruffled tail dangling —
abruptly wasted and died of liver failure: We buried him
this morning by the barn, in the cat's graveyard
under blue asters, tamping dirt down over a last red ear.
Downstairs her nieces gather weeping among soft chairs

24

while neighbors bring casseroles and silence;
in the bedroom the widower opens the closet door
where her dresses hang, and finds one hanger swaying.
At Blackwater Farm beside Route 4 the vale bellies
wide from the river, four hundred acres of black dirt

25

over glacial sand, where Jack and his uncles spread
a century of cow manure. They milked their cattle
morning and night, feeding them grain, silage, and hay
while the renewable sisters drank at the river's edge,
chewed cuds, bore yearly calves, bounced and mooed

26

to praise each other's calving, and produced a frothing
blue-white Atlantic of Holstein milk. Yesterday the roads
went in, great yellow earthmachines dozing through loam
to sand, as Jack's boy Richard raises fifty Colonial Capes
with two-car garages and driveways, RIVERVIEW MEADOW FARMS

27

over smothered alluvial soil. "Death tends to occur,"
as the Professor actually said, "at the end of life."
When I heard that his daughter coming home from her job
found Clarence cold in his bed, I remembered the veiny
cheeks and laconic stories: For one moment I mourned him.

28

Then I felt my lungs inflate themselves deeply, painfully:
I imagined my own body beneath the disordered quilt.
For the first time in a year I felt myself collapse
under the desire to smoke. Like you, I want to die:
We praise death when we smoke, and when we stop smoking.

29

After the farmer fired him, the drunk farmhand returned
at nightfall and beat him to death with a tire iron
while his wife and six-year-old son stood watching.
As his father's body flopped in the wet sand, as blood
coiled out of ears, the boy — who had observed

30

hens without heads, stuck pigs, and a paralyzed mule
twitching in a stall — cried, "Die! Please die. Please."
Let us praise St. Nihil's Church of the Suburban Consensus;
at St. Nihil's we keep the coffin closed for the funeral;
when we take communion at St. Nihil's, the Euphemism melts

31

in our mouths: *pass, pass away, sleep, decease, expire.*
Quickly by shocking fire that blackens and vanishes,

turning insides out, or slowly by fires of rust and rot,
the old houses die, the barns and outbuildings die.
Let us praise death that removes nails carpenters hammered

32

during the battle of Shiloh; that solves the beam-shape
an adze gave an oak tree; that collapses finally
the settler's roof into his root cellar, where timber sawn
two centuries ago rots among weeds and saplings. Let us
praise death for the house erected by skill and oxen.

33

Let us praise death in old age. Wagging our tails,
bowing, whimpering, let us praise sudden crib-death
and death in battle: Dressed in blue the rifleman charges
the granite wall. Let us praise airplane crashes.
We buried thirty-year-old Stephen the photographer

34

in Michigan's November rain. His bony widow Sarah, pale
in her loose black dress, leaned forward impulsively
as the coffin, suspended from a yellow crane, swayed
over the hole. When she touched the shiny damp maple
of the box, it swung slightly away from her

35

as it continued downward. Stephen's mother Joan
knelt first to scrape wet dirt onto the coffin lid;
then his father Peter lifted handfuls and let them drop,
then his sister Sarah, then his widow Sarah. Under
scraggly graveyard trees, five young gravediggers stood

36

smoking together, men tattooed and unshaven, wearing
baseball caps, shifting from foot to foot, saying
nothing, trying never to watch in Michigan's November rain.
"Bitterly, bitterly I weep for my blood-brother Enkidu.
Should I *praise* master death that commanded my friend?

37
"I wander hunting in the forest weeping salt tears;
in my anger I slaughter the deer. Bitterly I cry:
'Nowhere can I lay my head down to rest or to sleep!
Despair sucks my liver out! Desolation eats bitter meat
from my thigh! What happened to my brother will happen to me.'

38
"I stood by his body eight days. I implored him to throw
death over, to rise and pull his gold breastplate on.
On the ninth day worms crawled from the skin of his neck.
Now, therefore, I climb to the sun's garden, to Utnapishtim
who alone of all men after the flood lives without dying."

Notes on OLD AND NEW POEMS

The last section (pages 195–236) contains the *New*. Older poems are largely derived from earlier books: *Exiles and Marriages* (1955), *The Dark Houses* (1958), *A Roof of Tiger Lilies* (1963), *The Alligator Bride* (1969), *The Yellow Room* (1971), *The Town of Hill* (1975), *Kicking the Leaves* (1978), a pamphlet *The Toy Bone* (1979), and *The Happy Man* (1986). Four older poems are collected for the first time: "The Hole," "Between the Clock and the Bed," "The Clown," and "President and Poet."

Several poems from the first three books, reprinted in *The Alligator Bride,* are omitted here; and I have included others that I left out then. Many poems remain unchanged. Others revised in 1969 are further revised here; some return to an earlier condition. The eldest words here go back to 1947, to "Old Home Week," but this poem is the proverbial very old axe. When I put "Old Home Day" in *Exiles and Marriages* in 1955, it had twelve lines; when I reprinted it in *The Alligator Bride* fourteen years later, I cut it to eight somewhat different lines; of the four printed here as "Old Home Week," I have altered two. Yet the fourth line was there in 1947.

Many readers dislike the notion that a sixty-year-old should alter language set down at eighteen, twenty-two, or for that matter fifty-three. I understand but I cannot resist. Although there are poems I am happy to omit, and others I reprint without change, when I look over old things I find a third category: I like much of a poem but some segment or piece of language repels me: I will not reprint the poem unless I can repair it.

"Old Home Week" (3) (also called "Old Home Day") was proclaimed by New Hampshire's governor in 1899, a holiday of reunion, acknowledging the rural diaspora.

"Exile" (8) was the Newdigate Prize Poem, Oxford, 1952.

"Christmas Eve in Whitneyville" (21–22). My father (1903–1955) died December 22 and was buried on December 24.

"A Second Stanza" (28). Samuel Johnson wrote the first stanza to demonstrate that verse was not poetry.

"The Scream," "Marat's Death," "The Kiss," and "Between the Clock and the Bed" (43–46) respond to paintings and woodcuts by Edvard Munch.

"Internal and External Forms," "King and Queen," and "Reclining Figure" (74–76) respond to sculpture by Henry Moore.

"O Flodden Field" (77–78). The phrase is inscribed in stone on the battlefield. The poem was written in memory of Edwin Muir.

"The Old Pilot" (80). In memory of Philip Thompson.

"Beau of the Dead" (80–81) is paraphrased and partly quoted from Henry James's *The Sense of the Past.*

"Letter to an English Poet" (84–85) is addressed to Charles Tomlinson.

"Old Houses" (98–99) uses phrases from T. E. Hulme's notebooks.

"The Town of Hill" (123–124). The old town of Hill, New Hampshire, was evacuated in the early 1940s in a flood control project.

"Flies" (144–147). In memory of Kate Keneston Wells, 1878–1975.

"Old Timers' Day" (177–178). Ted Williams wore number nine.

"Edward's Anecdote" (202–204) repeats, in different language, an anecdote from a poem by Ellen Bryant Voigt.

"Notes for Nobody" (214–215). In 1959 I interviewed Henry Moore for *Horizon;* in 1965 I did his *New Yorker* profile.

"Praise for Death" (229–236) ends paraphrasing some lines from *Gilgamesh.* Gilgamesh was the king of Uruk mentioned in the fifth stanza.

In *The Happy Man* and *The One Day,* I thanked friends who helped me with my poems; I thank them again. Because this book collects poems written over forty years, I would list dozens of names if I were to take account of everyone who helped. I must take refuge in a general gratitude.

For this selection I have mostly relied on the help of eight people: Jane Kenyon, Cynthia Huntington, Liam Rector, Frank Bidart, Robert Pinsky, Robert Bly, Galway Kinnell, and Peter Davison.

INDEX OF TITLES AND FIRST LINES

Titles are set in italic type.

A bear sleeps in a cellarhole; pine
    needles, 70
Abraham Lincoln was giggling
    uncontrollably, 119
Abroad Thoughts from Home, 29
A coal fire burned in a basket grate,
    100
Acorns, 187
Adultery at Forty, 131
A fly sleeps on the field of a green
    curtain, 144
After fifty years Amelia Earhart's
    Lockheed fretted with rust, 213
After the many courses, hot bowls of
    rice, 141
Against the bright, 178
Against the clapboards and the
    window panes, 14
Airstrip in Essex 1960, An, 69
Alligator Bride, The, 96
All winter your brute shoulders
    strained against collars, padding,
    158
Although the car radio warned that,
    217
And now September burns the
    careful tree, 6
An oak twig drops, 187
An old *Life* photograph, 182
Apples, 103
A rock drops in a bucket, 109
As the last light, 168
As they grew older, 75
At Delphi, 11
At Delphi where the eagles climb, 11
At fourteen, parked, 211

"At pet stores in Detroit, you can
    buy, 116
At the edge of the city the pickerel,
    68
At the shower's head, high over the
    porcelain moonscape, 131
August, goldenrod blowing. We
    walk, 127
A woman who lived, 64

Back of the dam, under, 123
Baseball Players, The, 178
Beau of the Dead, 80
"Beginning at five o'clock,
    just before dawn rises, 191
Beside the door, 13
Between pond and sheepbarn, by
    maples and watery birches, 181
"Between the Clock and the Bed,"
    45
Black-faced Sheep, The, 156
Blue Wing, The, 101
Body Politic, The, 27
Bowing he asks her the favor, 25
Brief Lives, 208
By the Exeter River, 33
By the road to church, Shaker
    Village, 49

Carlotta's Confession, 204
Carol, A, 209
Charlotte, "the angel of assass-, 44
Child, The, 65
Child's Garden, A, 4
Christ Church Meadows, 46
Christmas Eve in Whitneyville, 21
Cider 5¢ A Glass, 197
Clown, The, 47

Coal Fire, The, 100
Coffee Cup, The, 222
Cold Water, 78
Columns of the Parthenon, The, 12
Conduct and Work, 19
Cops and Robbers, 23
Corner, The, 93

Dancers, 25
Day I Was Older, The, 186
Days, The, 89
December, and the closing of the
    year, 21
December, nightfall at three-thirty,
    94
Digging, 76
Driving back from the market, 118
Dump, The, 110

Each of us waking to the window's
    light, 8
Eating the Pig, 135
Edward's Anecdote, 202
Eleanor's Letters, 120
Elegy for Wesley Wells, 14
Even the dignity of Christ, 20
Every year the mountains, 175
Exile, 8

Family, The, 53
Farm, The, 61
Fathers and Sons, 30
Festival lights go on, 119
Fête, 119
Flies, 144
For an Exchange of Rings, 188
For five years of my life, or ten, 112
Foundations of American Industry,
    The, 50
Friend Revisited, A, 13
From that daye thee Hart strokys, 176
From the dark yard by the sheepbarn
    the cock crowed, 166

Glass, air, ice, light, 38

God, I know nothing, my sense is all
    nonsense, 210
Gold, 109
Grace, A, 210
Granite and Grass, 179
Granted that what we summon is
    absurd, 48
Grave the Well, The, 97
Great blue mountain! Ghost, 106
Great Day in the Cows' House, 163
Green Shelf, The, 118
Grown-ups, The, 55

Hang it all, Ezra Pound, there is only
    the one sestina, 41
He could remember that in the past,
    seven months ago, 23
He discovers himself on an old
    airfield, 80
He lives among a dog, 65
Henyard Round, The, 166
"He played jacks with me, 170
Here is a fat animal, a bear, 71
"Here she comes, 99
He steps around a gate of bushes,
    78
He suspects that the seasons, 42
He waited in the sadness of the sun's
    intention, 65
He walks out of the village. The
    road, 81
High on a slope in New Guinea, 93
High Pasture, The, 113
Hole, The, 23
Hut of the Man Alone, The, 35

I am dead, to be sure, 31
I am the hounds, 113
Idea of Flying, The, 63
I drank cool water from the fountain,
    121
I have visited Men's Rooms, 102
I lived in a dry well, 67
I lived no-color. In a gray room I
    talked, 112
Illustration, 130

I look at the rock and the house, 114
Impossible Marriage, The, 189
I'm sure I can't remember where, but some, 4
In a bookshelf at the dark living room's end, 130
"In mid-August, in the second year, 139
In nineteen-thirty-four we spent July, 37
In October of the year, 147
"Internal and External Forms," 74
In the dark tie-up seven huge Holsteins, 163
In the Ford plant, 50
In the Great Hall where Lady Ann by firelight after dining alone, 177
In the Kitchen of the Old House, 88
In the kitchen of the old house, late, 88
In the middle distance, 62
In the nap there are numerous doors, boudoirs, a talking hall, 216
In the pantry the dear dense cheeses, Cheddars and harsh, 131
In the shaft graves, butterflies, 72
In the yellow light, an old man, 45
I put my hat upon my head, 28
I remember watching, 67
I shot my friend to save my country's life, 27
It discovers by night, 62
It does not know, 93
It has happened suddenly, 32
It is a lost road into the air, 69
it is an accurate nose, 111
It is not in the books, 39
It keeps out everything! It goes, 34
I was sleeping in Madison, Anthony Bradbury's spare room, 213
"I was twelve when my father gave me this .22, 192
I who picked up the neat, 120

Jack Baker, 221
Jealous Lovers, 73

Jerome had lived alone for thirty years, 35
Je Suis une Table, 32
John Fleming walked in the house his cousin left him, 80

Kicking the Leaves, 132
Kicking the leaves, October, as we walk home together, 132
Kill, The, 66
"King and Queen," 75
"Kiss, The," 44

Lady, what are you laughing at? Is it the joke, 55
"Late one night she told me, 202
Late snow fell this early morning of spring, 4
Letter to an English Poet, 84
Let us praise death that turns pink cheeks to ashes, 229
Like an oarless boat through midnight's watery, 212
Lone Ranger, The, 12
Long River, The, 59
Looking through boxes, 129
Love Is Like Sounds, 4

Man in the Dead Machine, The, 93
Maple Syrup, 127
"Marat's Death," 44
Match, 212
Material, 211
Maundy Thursday's Candles, 210
Merle Bascom's .22, 192
Milkers Broken Up, 213
Mime the loud wind in pain, 29
Mirror, mirror on the wall, 19
Mr. and Mrs. Billings, 52
Mr. Wakeville on Interstate 90, 190
Moon, The, 64
Moon Clock, 212
Mount Kearsarge, 106
Mycenae, 72
My Friend Felix, 191

"My grandfather's name was
    Augusto, 204
My history extends, 29
My Son My Executioner, 19
My son, my executioner, 19
My whole life has led me here, 102

Names of Horses, 158
New Animals, 169
New Hampshire, 70
1934, 37
No Color Man, 112
No Deposit, 26
No Deposit   No Return, 26
Nose, 111
Notes for Nobody, 214
Now it is gone, all of it, 112
"Now I will abandon the route of my
    life, 190

Observe. Ridged, raised, tactile, the
    horror, 43
O Cheese, 131
"*O Flodden Field*," 77
Often I saw, as on my balcony, 46
Old Home Week, 3
Old Houses, 98
Old houses were scaffolding once, 98
Old man remembers to old man, 3
Old Pilot, The, 80
Old Roses, 153
Old Timers' Day, 177
On a Horse Carved in Wood, 72
One midnight, after a day when
    lilies, 76
On Ragged Mountain birches twist
    from rifts in granite, 179
*On Reaching the Age of Two
    Hundred*, 143
Our Walk in Yorkshire, 209
Over my bed, 30
Ox Cart Man, 147
Oysters and Hermits, 36

Pale gold of the walls, gold, 109
Passage to Worship, 7

Persistence of 1937, 213
Photographs of China, 141
Pictures of Philippa, 99
Poem, The, 62
Poem with One Fact, 116
"Practically all you newspaper
    people," 47
Praise for Death, 229
President and Poet, 48
Presidentiad, The, 119

Raisin, The, 121
"*Reclining Figure*," 76
Red Branch, The, 20
Religious Articles, 49
Repeated Shapes, The, 102
Revolution, The, 177
Rocker, The, 170
Ruminant pillows! Gregarious soft
    boulders!, 156

Scenic View, 175
"*Scream, The*," 43
Sea, The, 67
Second Stanza, A, 28
Self-portrait As a Bear, 71
September Ode, 6
Sestina, 41
Set of Seasons, A, 42
Sew, 98
Sheep move on the grass, 66
Sheep mutter as we pass, 209
She is all around me, 101
She kneels on the floor, snip snip, 98
Shudder, 32
Sister by the Pond, A, 182
Sister on the Tracks, A, 181
Six Naps in One Day, 216
Sleeping, 74
Sleeping Giant, The, 24
Small Fig Tree, A, 31
Snow, The, 59
Snow is in the oak, 59
Snow starts at twilight. All night the
    house, 171
Some Oddities, 5

Southwest of Buffalo, 70
Speeches, 223
Standing on top of the hay, 61
Stones, 112
Stone Walls, 148
Stone walls emerge from leafy
  ground, 148
Stories, 114
Stump, 86
Sums, 176
Sun, The, 65
Swan, 94

Table, The, 104
Taking off from Kennedy, 97
Ten years ago this minute, he possibly
  sat, 89
The avenue rises toward a city of
  white marble, 74
The backs twist with the kiss, 44
The bride disappears. After twenty
  minutes of searching, 189
The clock of my days winds down, 96
The clock on the parlor wall, stout as
  a mariner's clock, 186
The first time I met him Henry Moore
  was sixty. Before tea, 214
The foot of death has printed on my
  chest, 32
The horses of the sea; remember, 72
The hugy spider stooping through the
  door, 5
The learned King fought, 77
The long lakes, flanked, 70
The musk ox smells, 59
The newspaper, the coffee cup,
  the dog's, 222
Then the knee of the wave, 76
The pock-marked player of the
  accordion, 3
The trolley has stopped long since,
  110
The warmth of cows, 209
The whole day long, under the
  walking sun, 24
The wings lacking a trunk, 63

The world is everything that is the
  case, 208
They have gone, 103
The young girls look up, 110
They rise into mind, 188
This Poem, 227
This poem is why, 227
Those several times she cleaved my
  dark, 7
Three Movements, The, 39
To a Waterfowl, 115
Today they cut down the oak, 86
Tomorrow, 217
To the Loud Wind, 29
Town of Hill, The, 123
Toy Bone, The, 129
Traffic, 153
Transcontinent, 122
Tree and the Cloud, The, 62
Trucks and station wagons, VWs, old
  Chevys, Pintos, 153
Tubes, 218
Twelve people, most of us strangers,
  stand in a room, 135
Twelve Seasons, 171
Two old men, 223

Umbrella, The, 34
Under the glassy Christmas tree, 53
Up and down the small streets,
  in which, 51
"Up, down, good, bad," said, 218

Valley of Morning, 221
Vast unmapped badlands spread
  without a road, 12
Village in East Anglia, A, 81

Waiting on the Corners, 38
Waking one morning, 169
Walking back to the farm from the
  depot, 104
Waters, 109
Wedding Party, 3
We live by love, but not by love
  alone, 36

Wells, 67
We speak the verses out of Mark, 210
"What is it you're mumbling, old
    Father, my Dad?, 33
What the birds say, 74
When he lies in the night away from
    her, 73
When I awoke on the morning, 143
When I go West you wear a marshal's
    star, 23
"When I heard Monica's, 197
when my father had been dead a
    week, 123
When the tall puffy, 177
Where the cities end, the, 122
Whip-poor-will, 168

White Apples, 123
White bone in the yellow flats of sun,
    12
White roses, tiny and old, flare
    among thorns, 153
Widows, The, 51
Wolf Knife, 139
Women with hats like the rear ends
    of pink ducks, 115
Woolworth's, 102
Wreckage, The, 68

Yellow fingers, 212
Young Watch Us, The, 110
Your letter describes, 84
"Your wife," the doctor said, 52